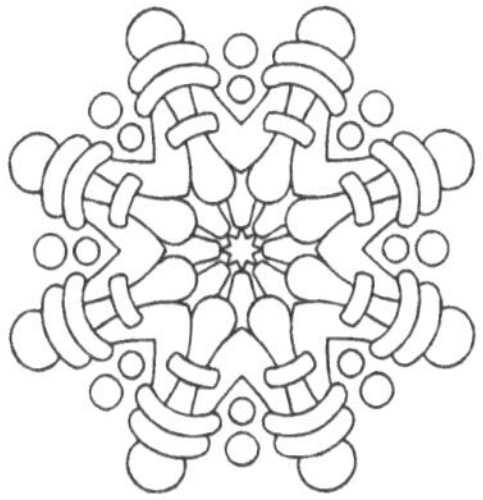

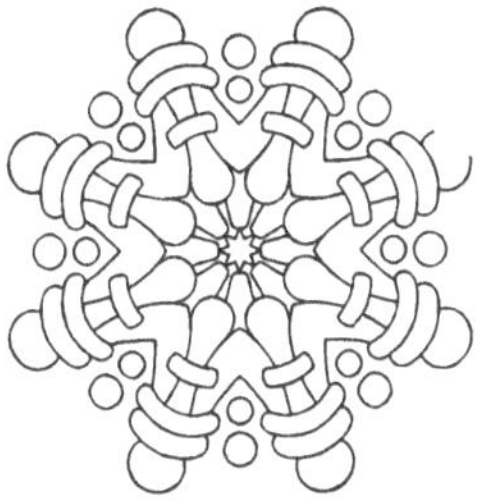

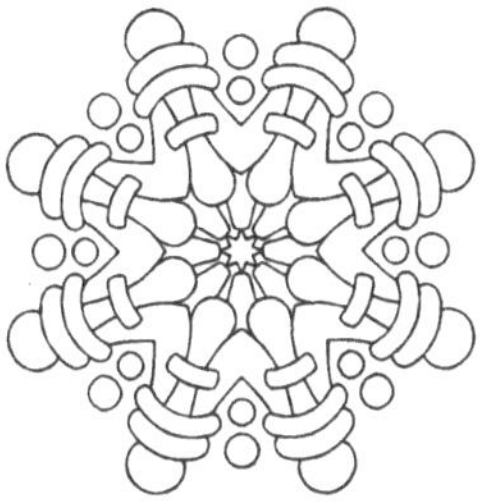

RELAXING POCKET PATTERNS

Lori's Pocket Pattern Coloring Books for Adults

VOLUME 2

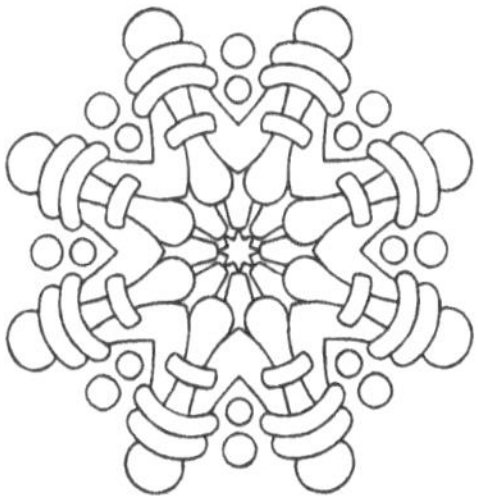

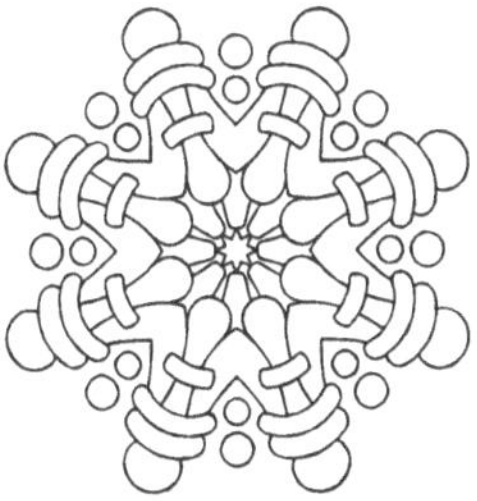

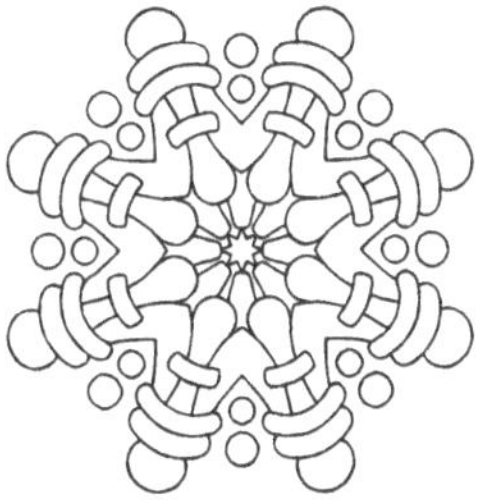

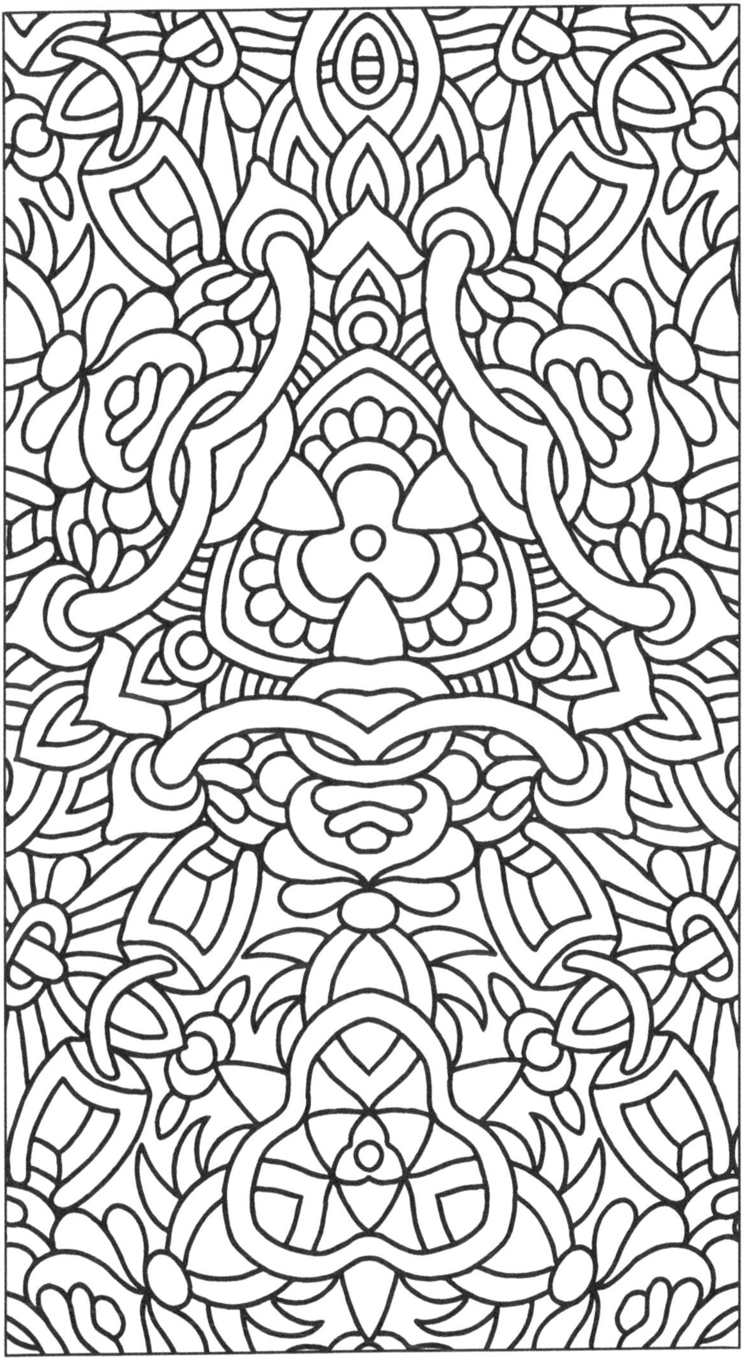

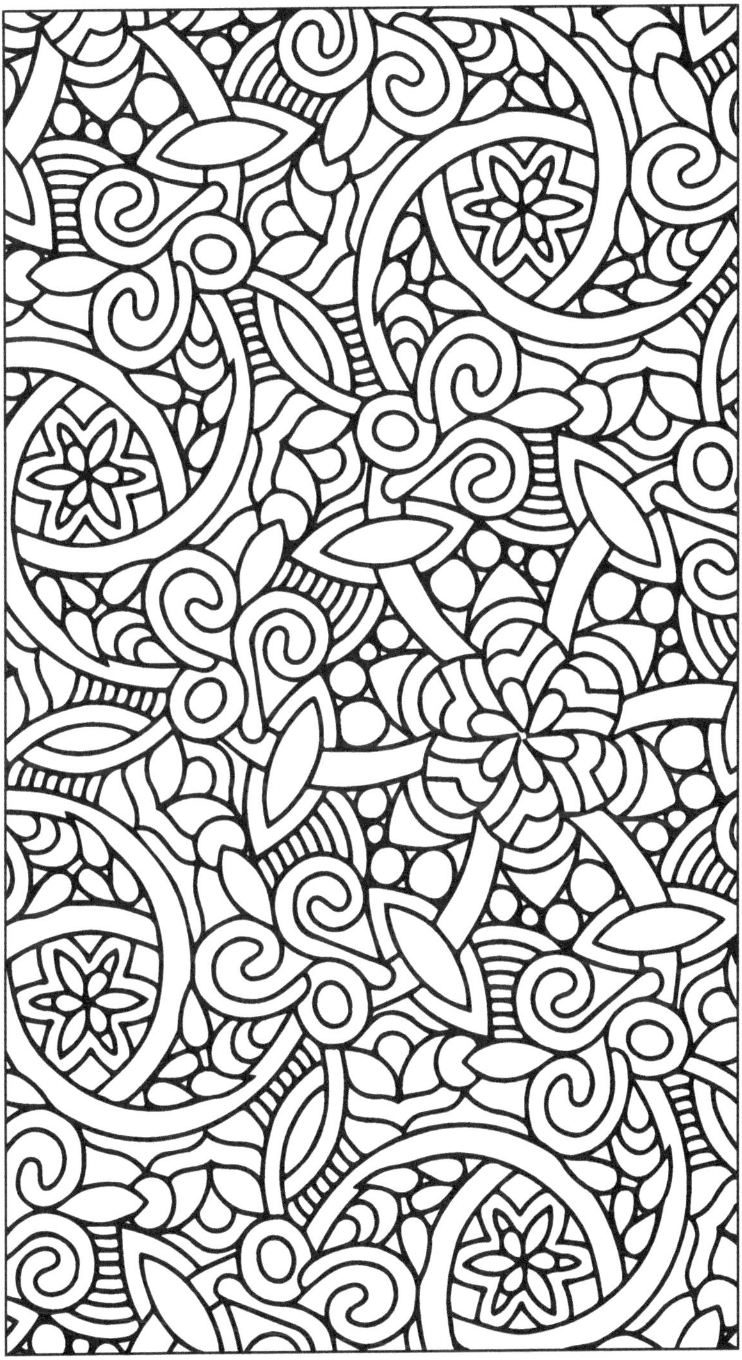

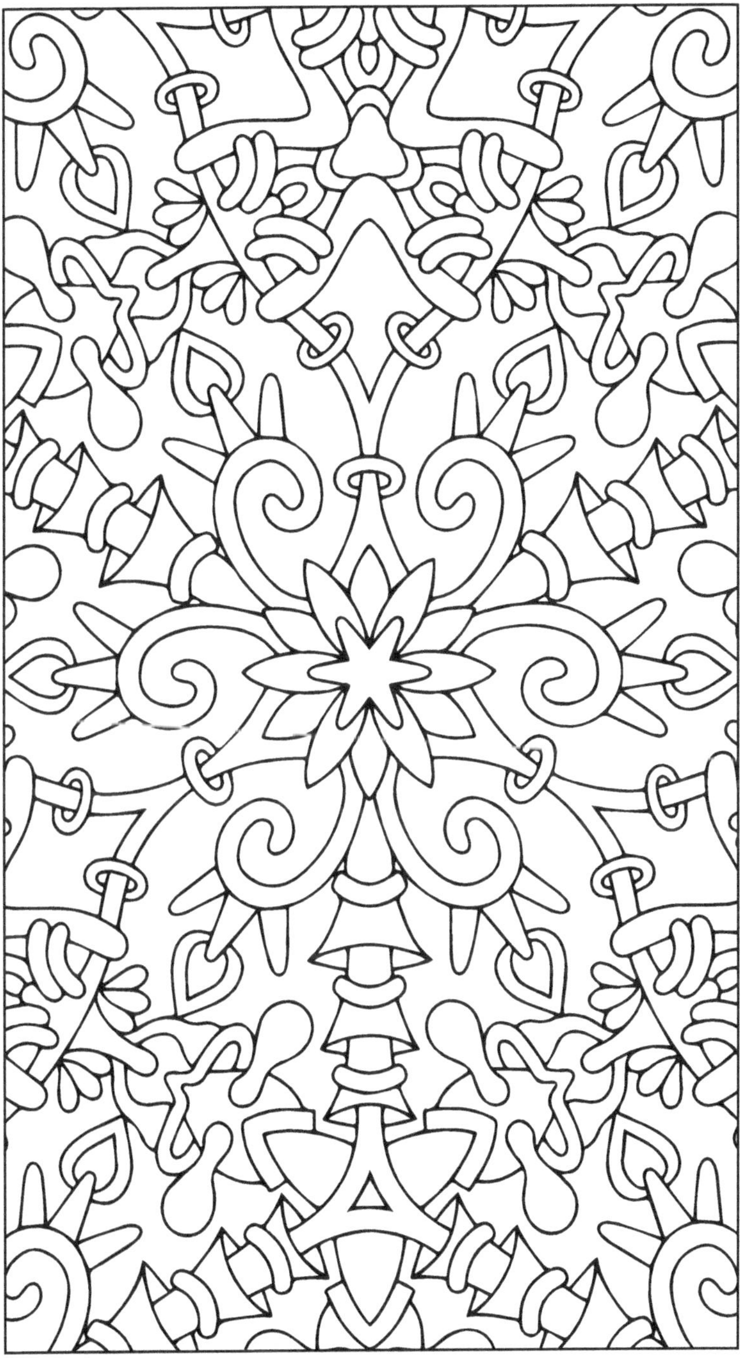

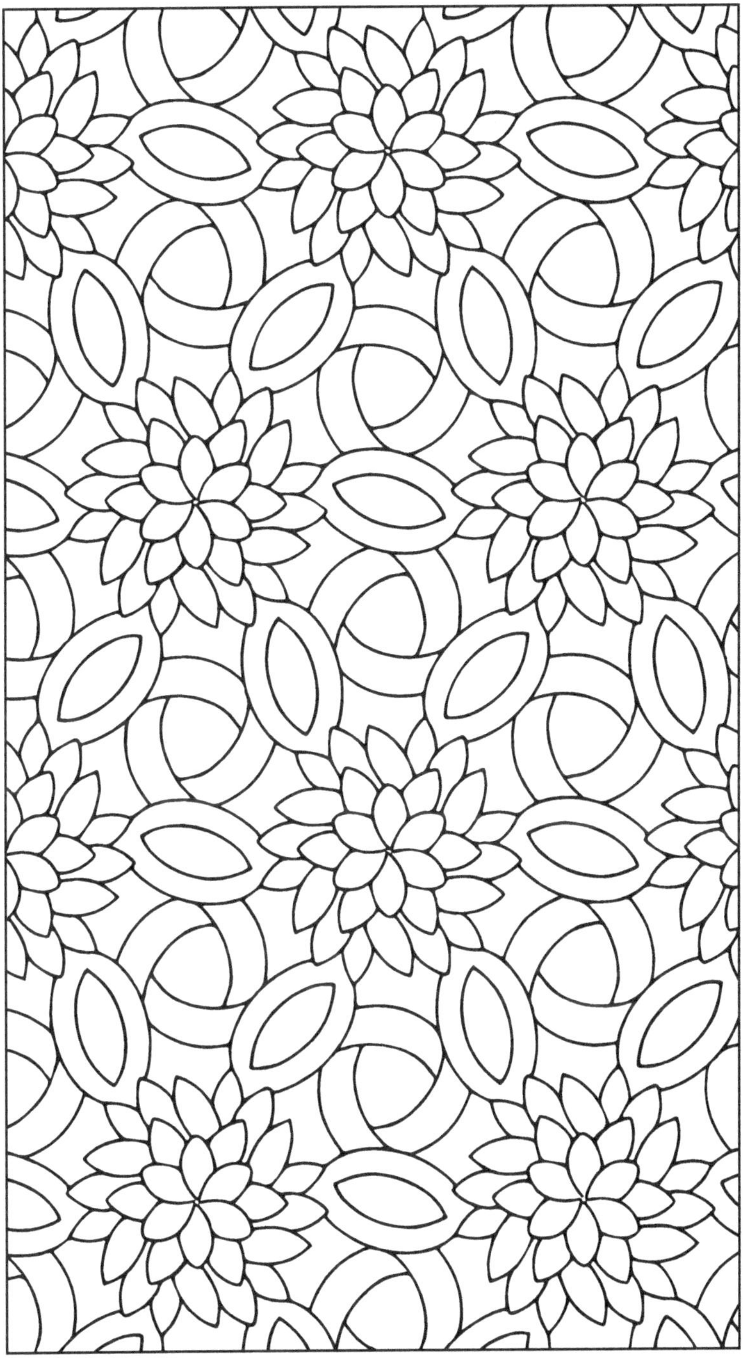

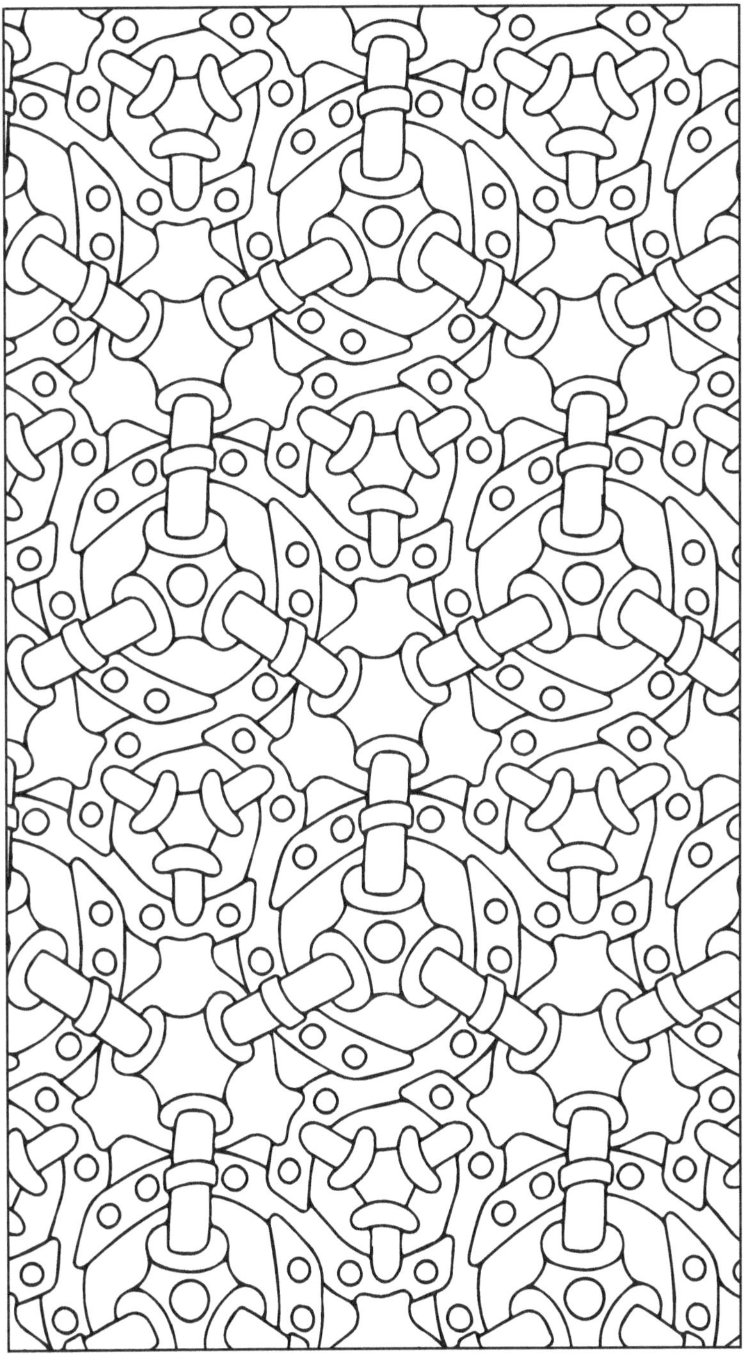

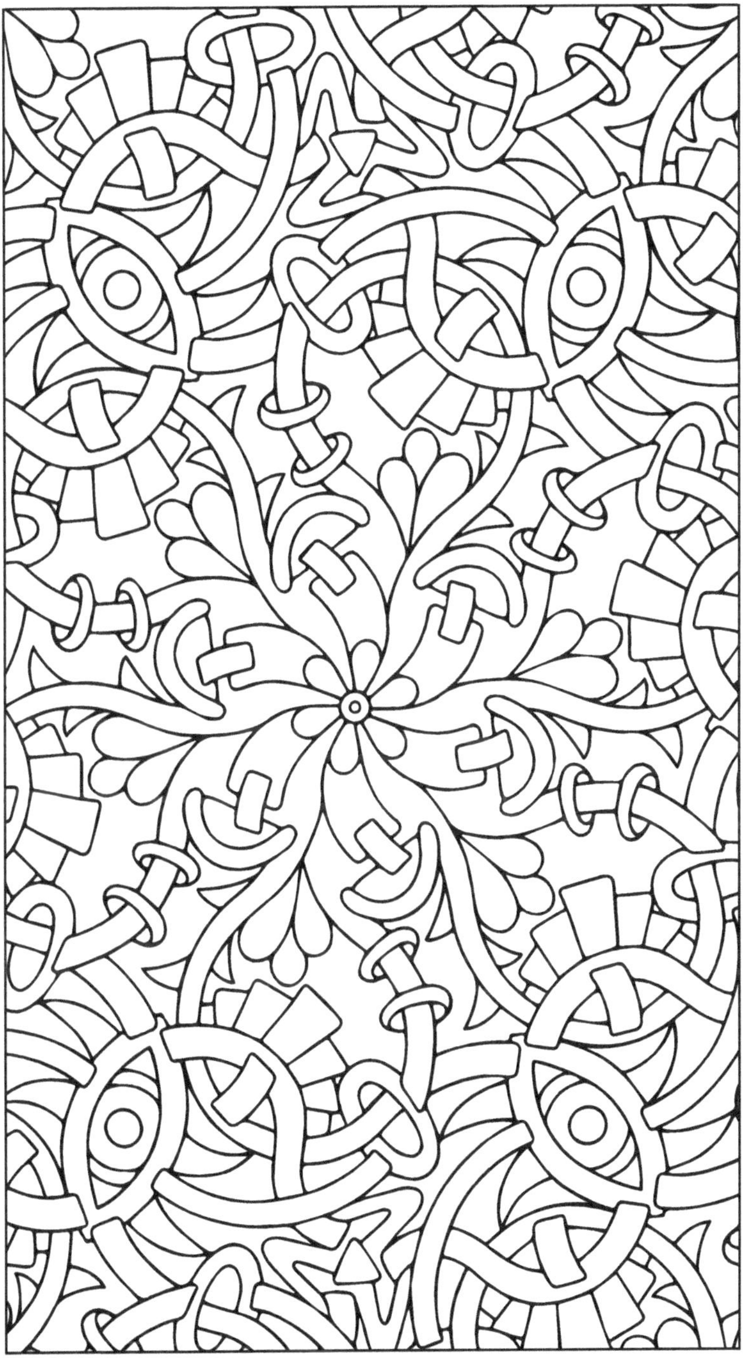

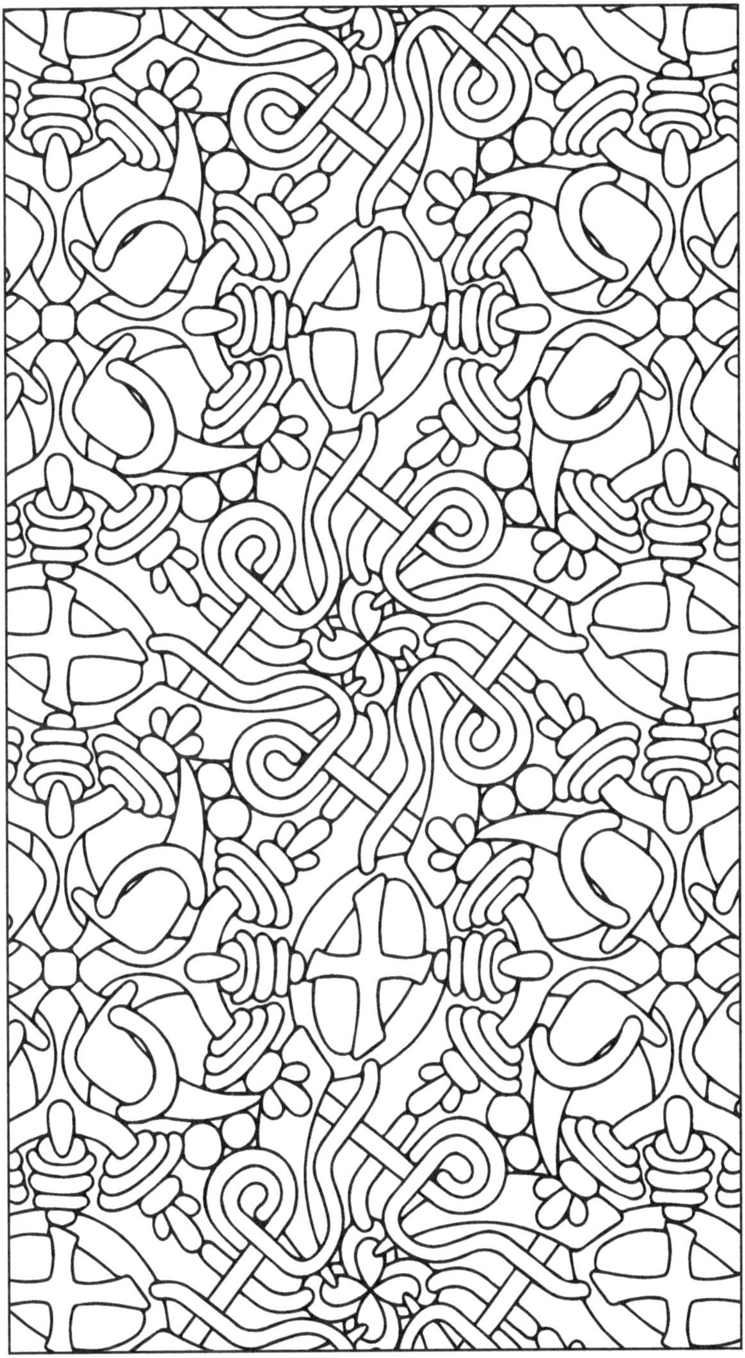

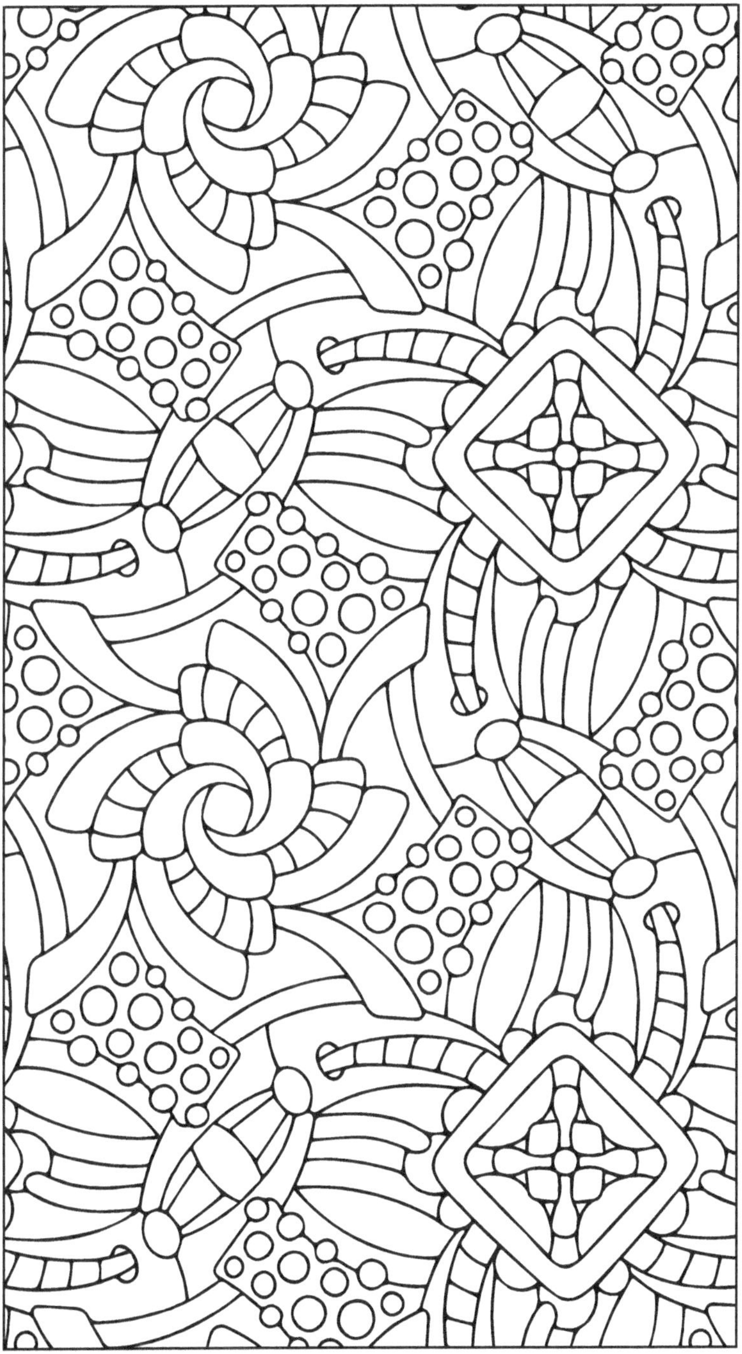

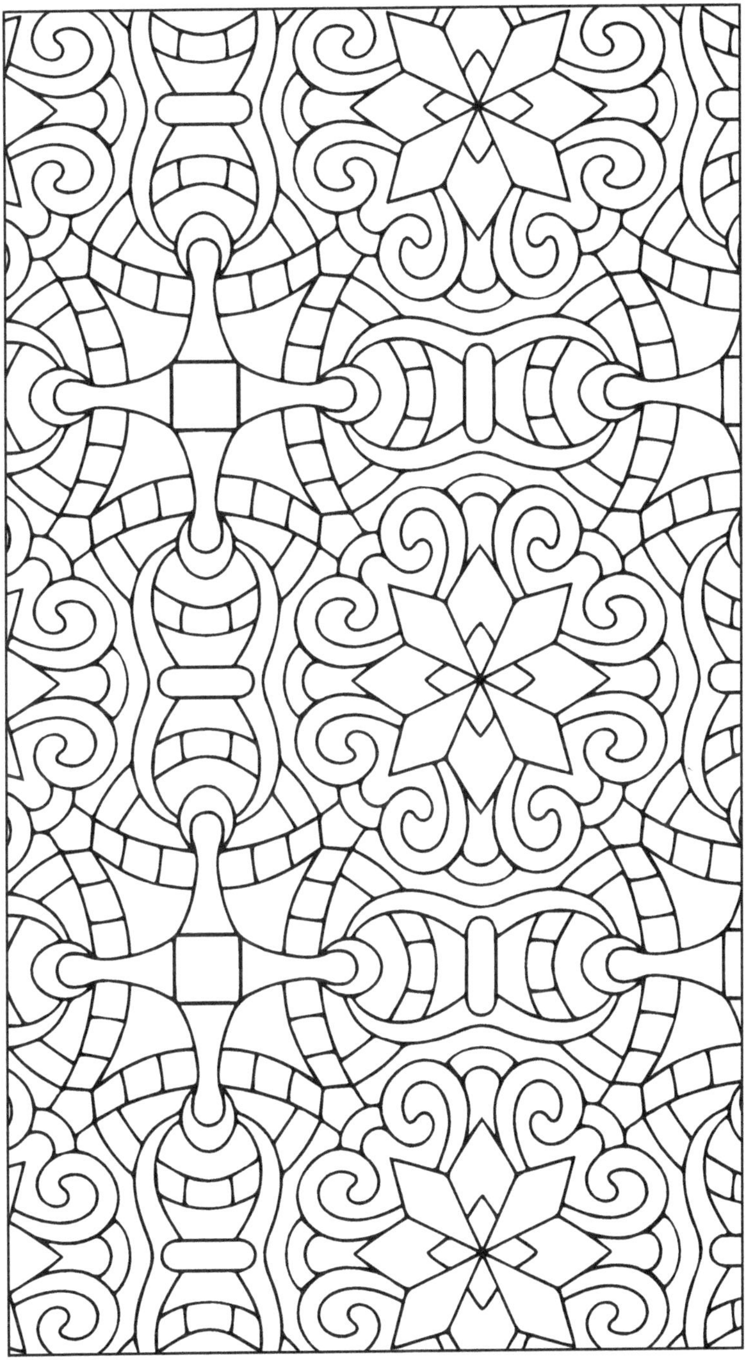

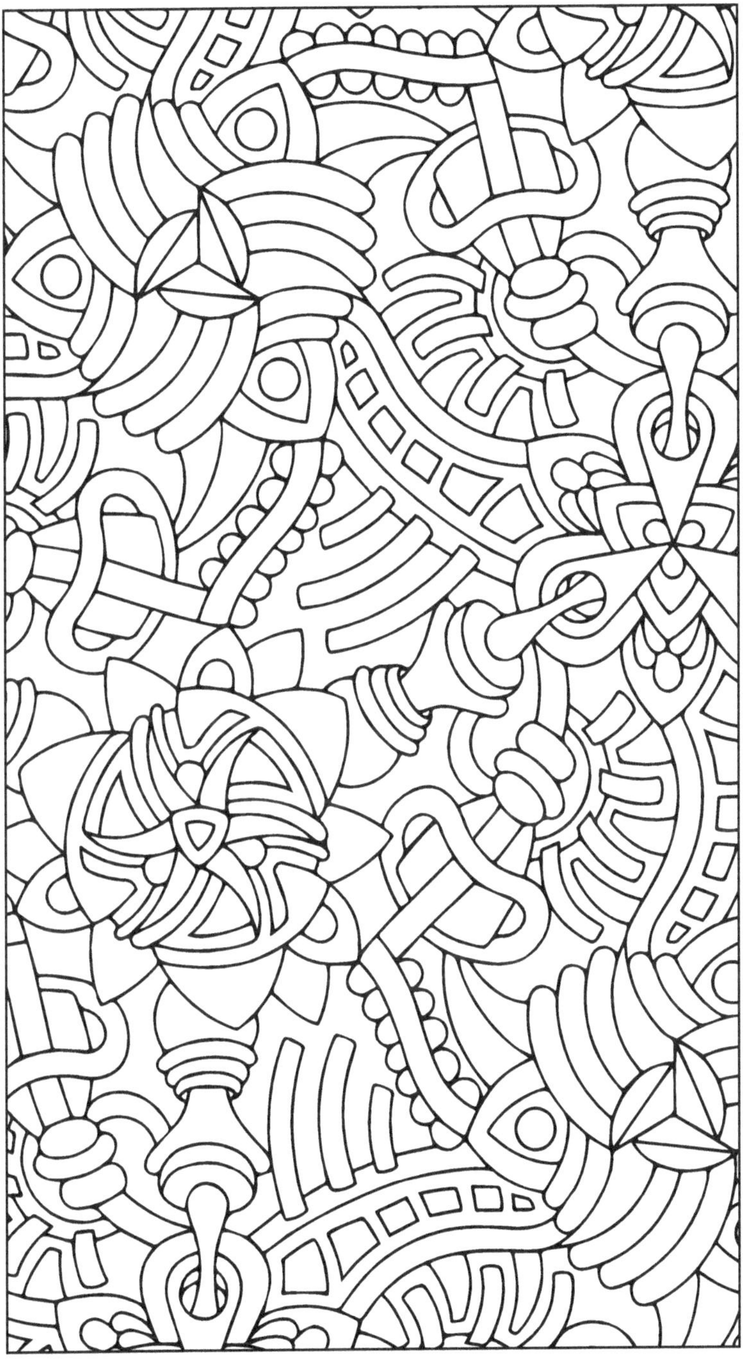

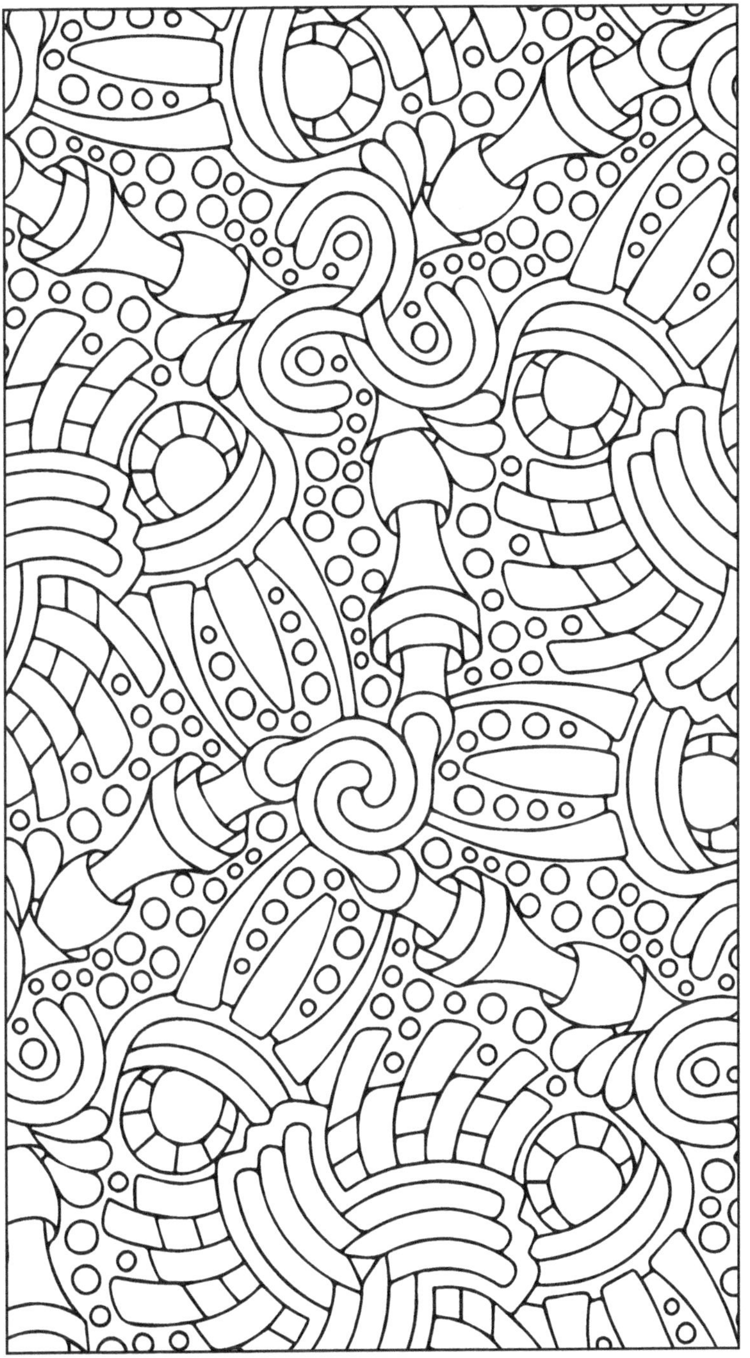

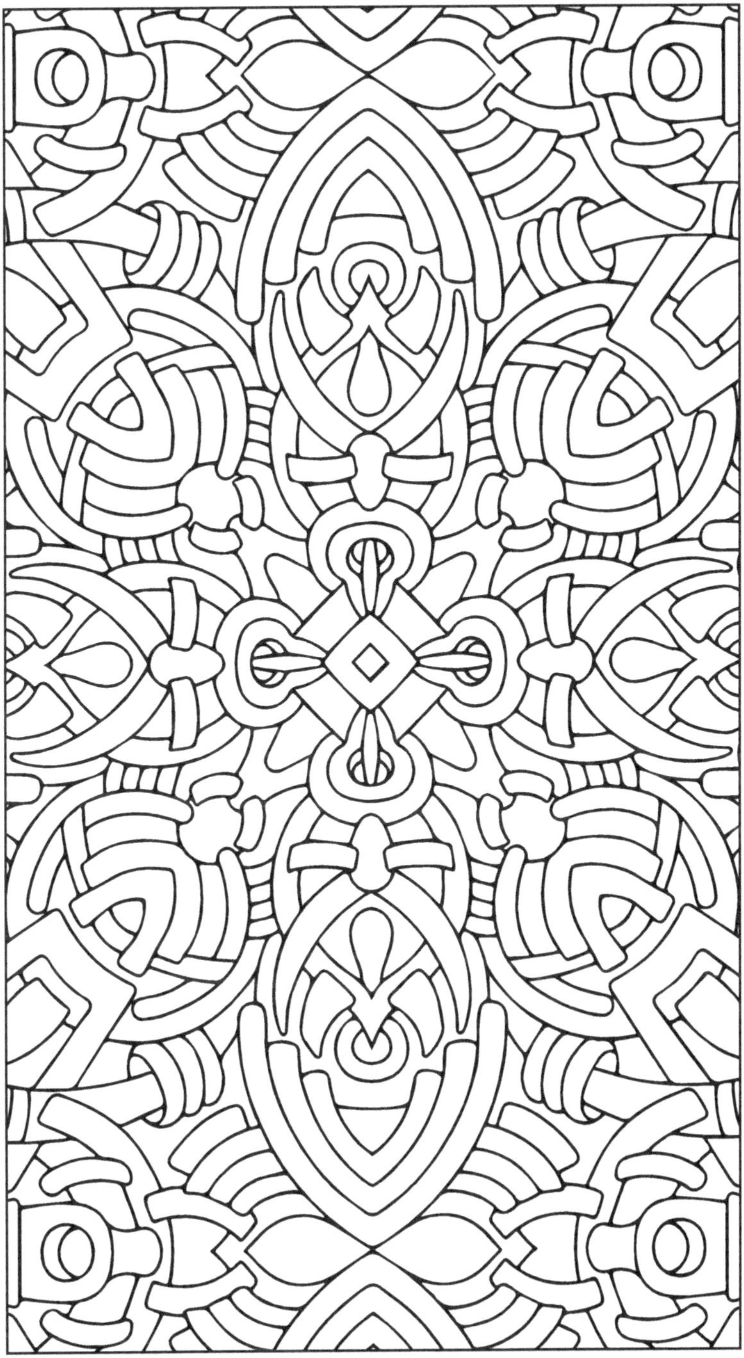

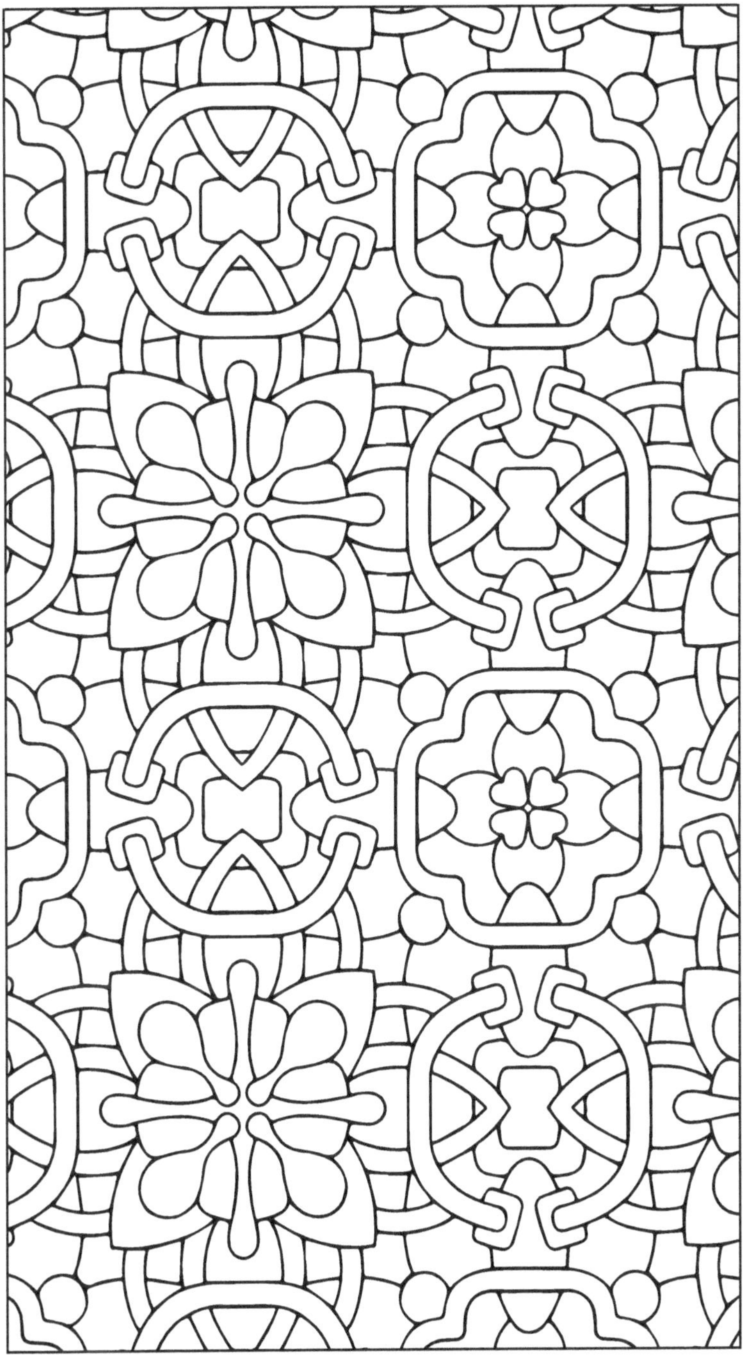

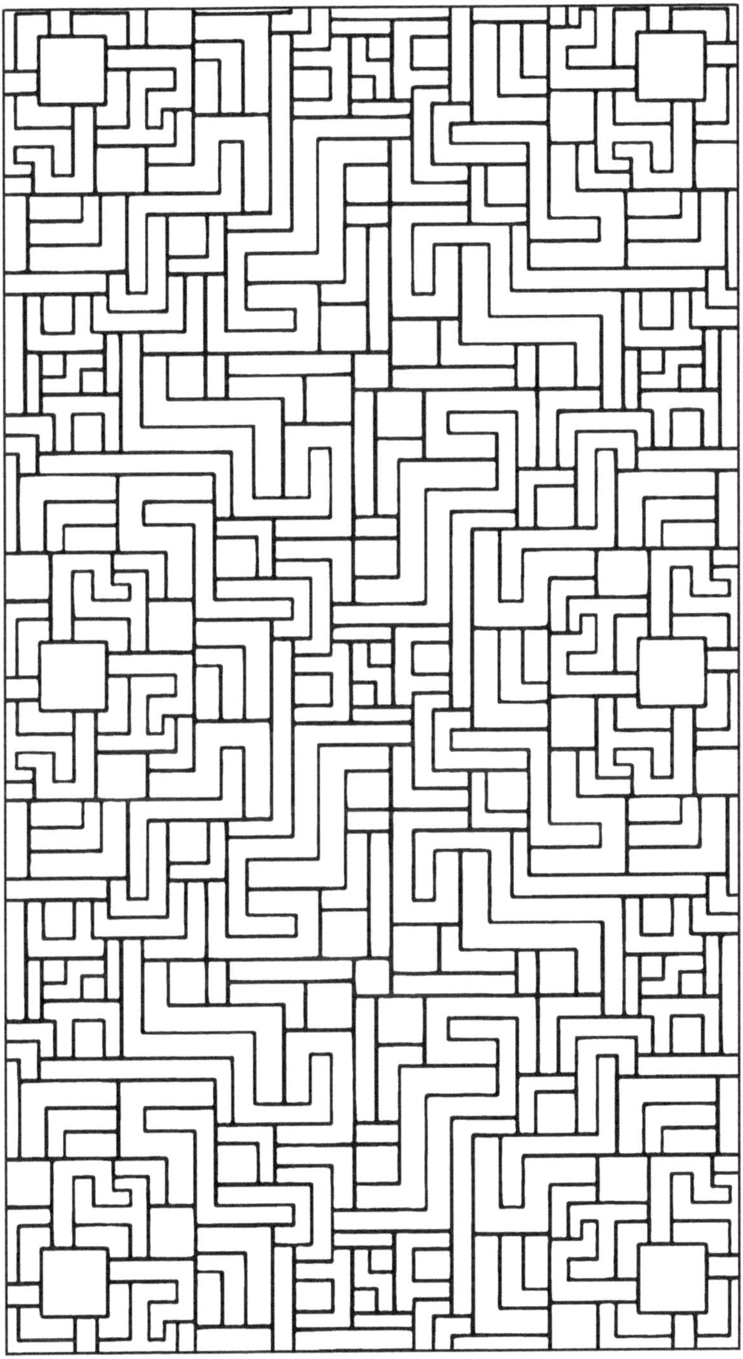

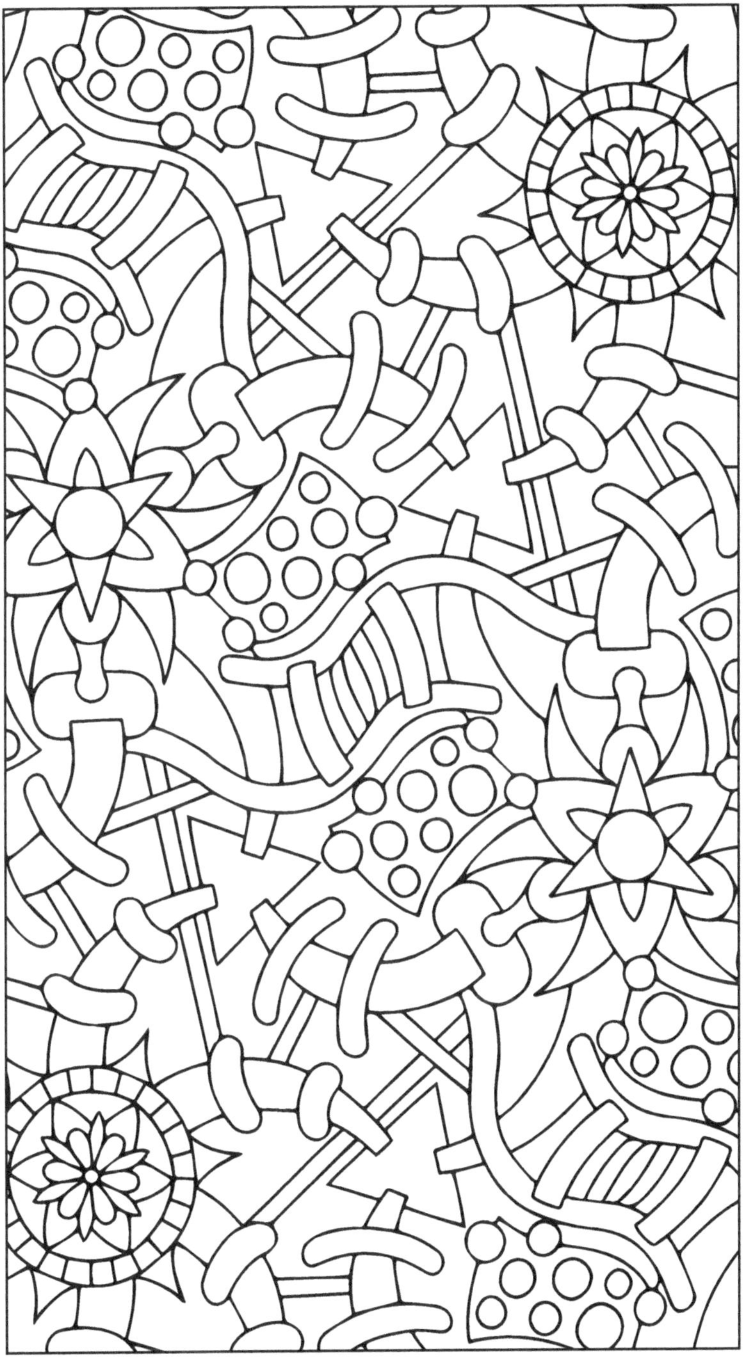

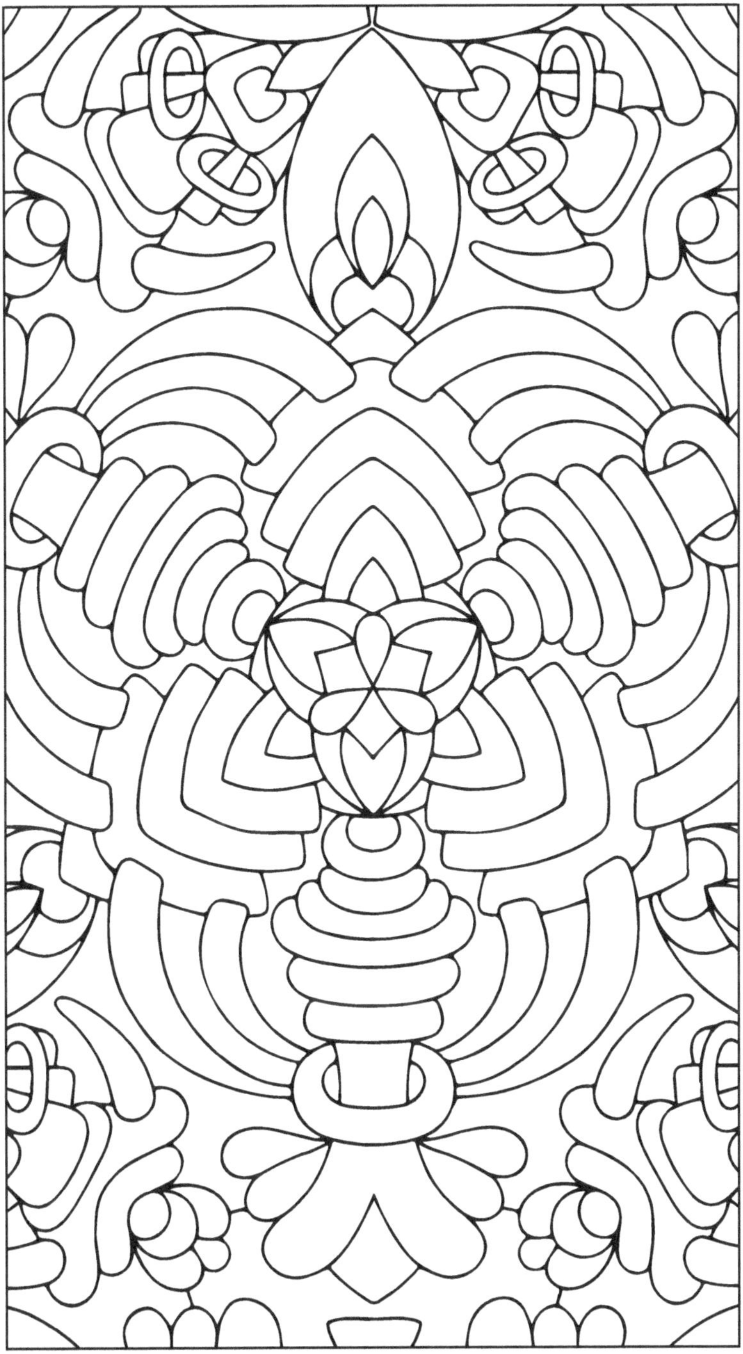

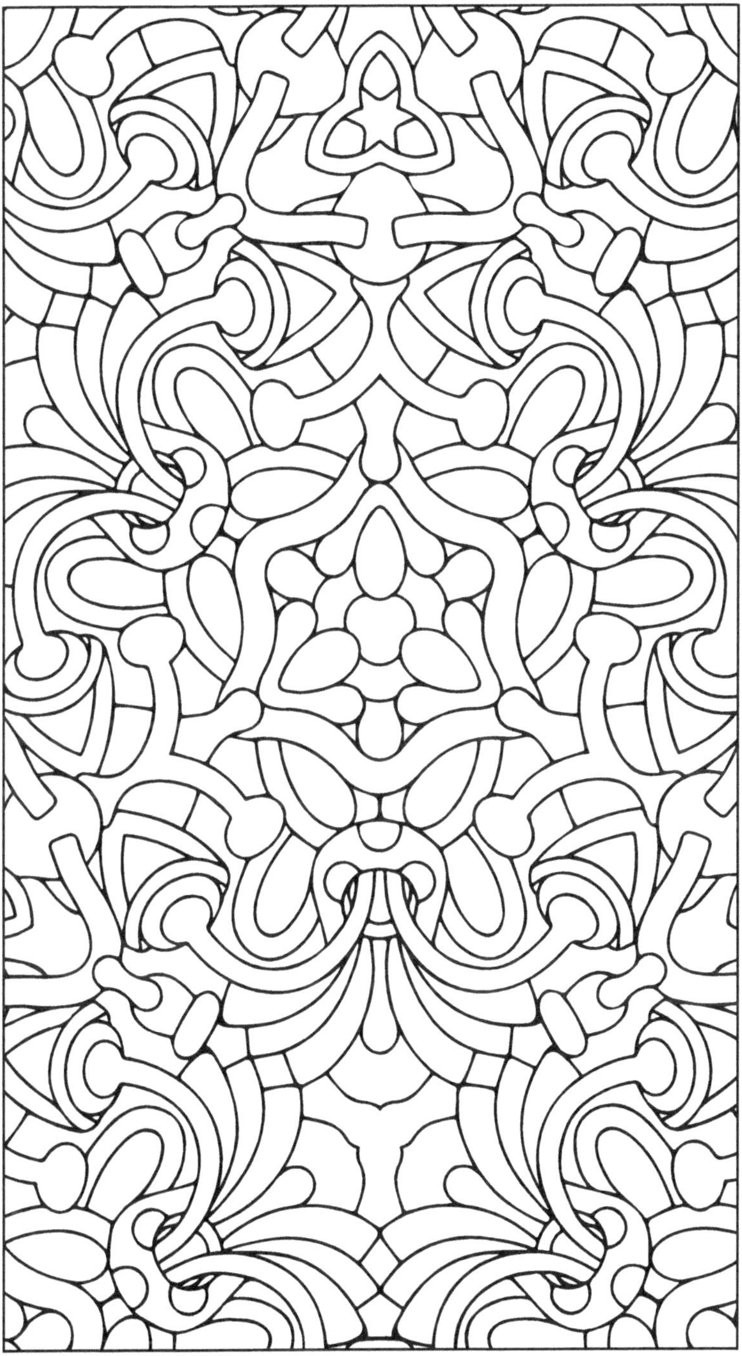

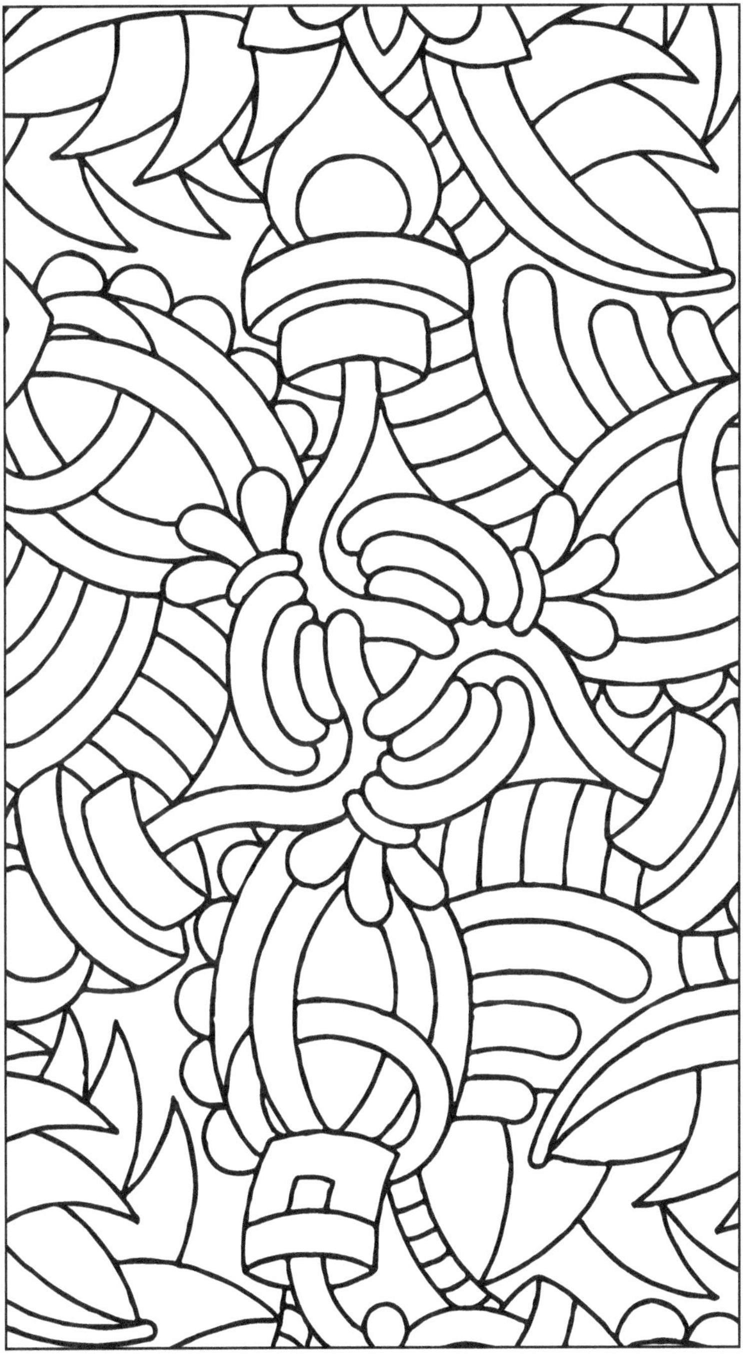

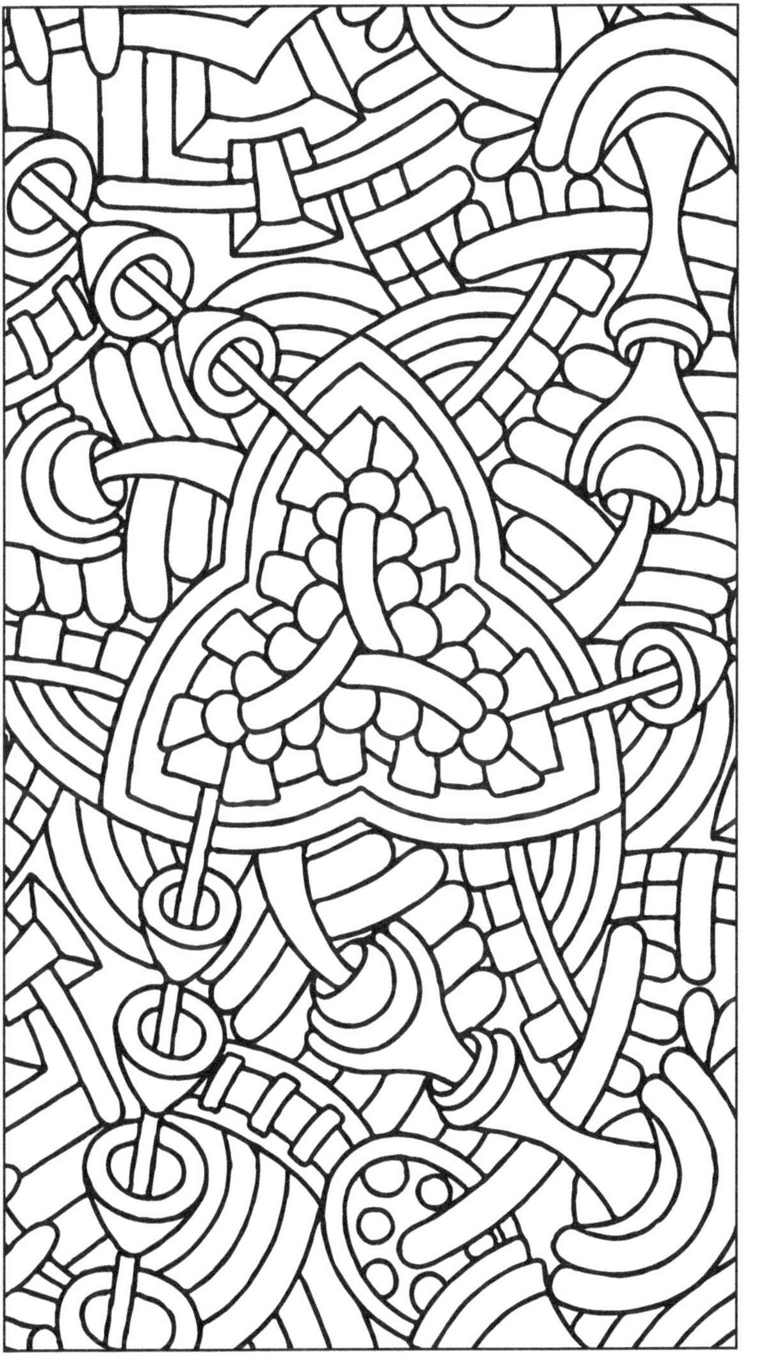

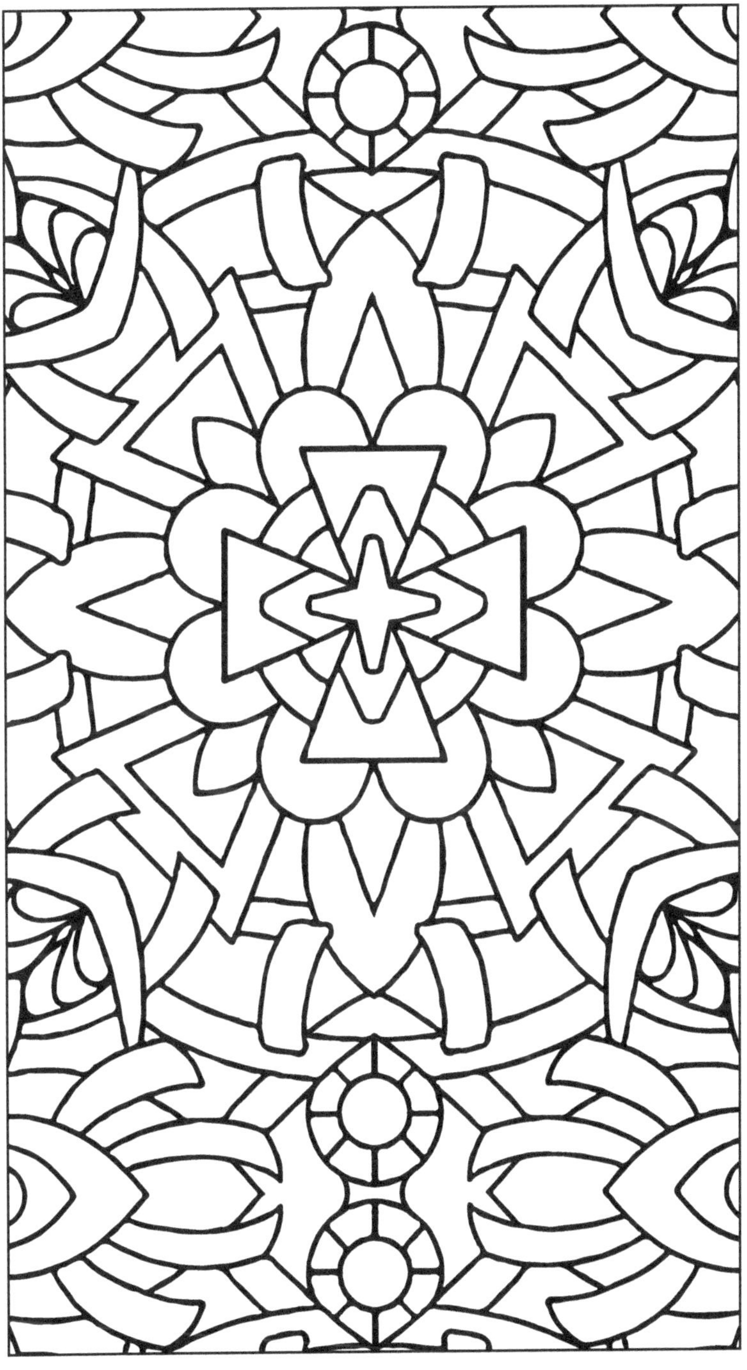

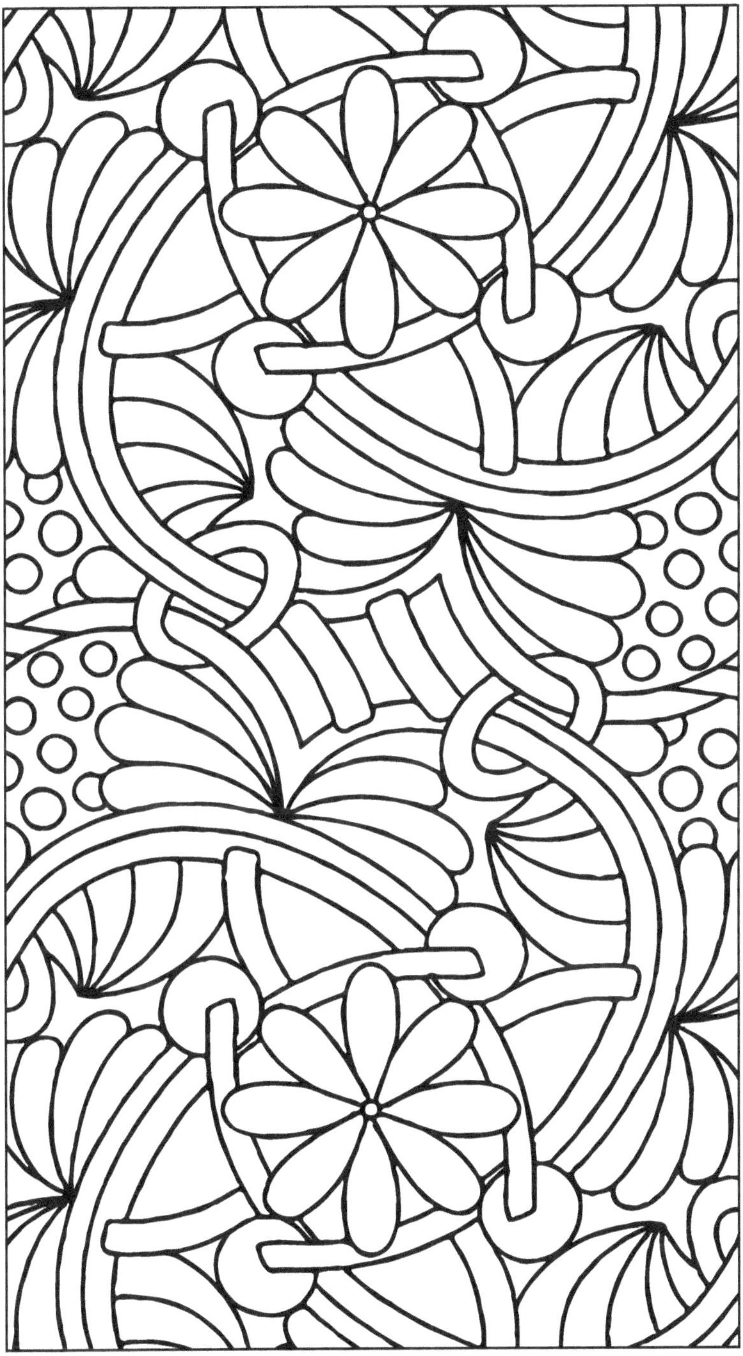

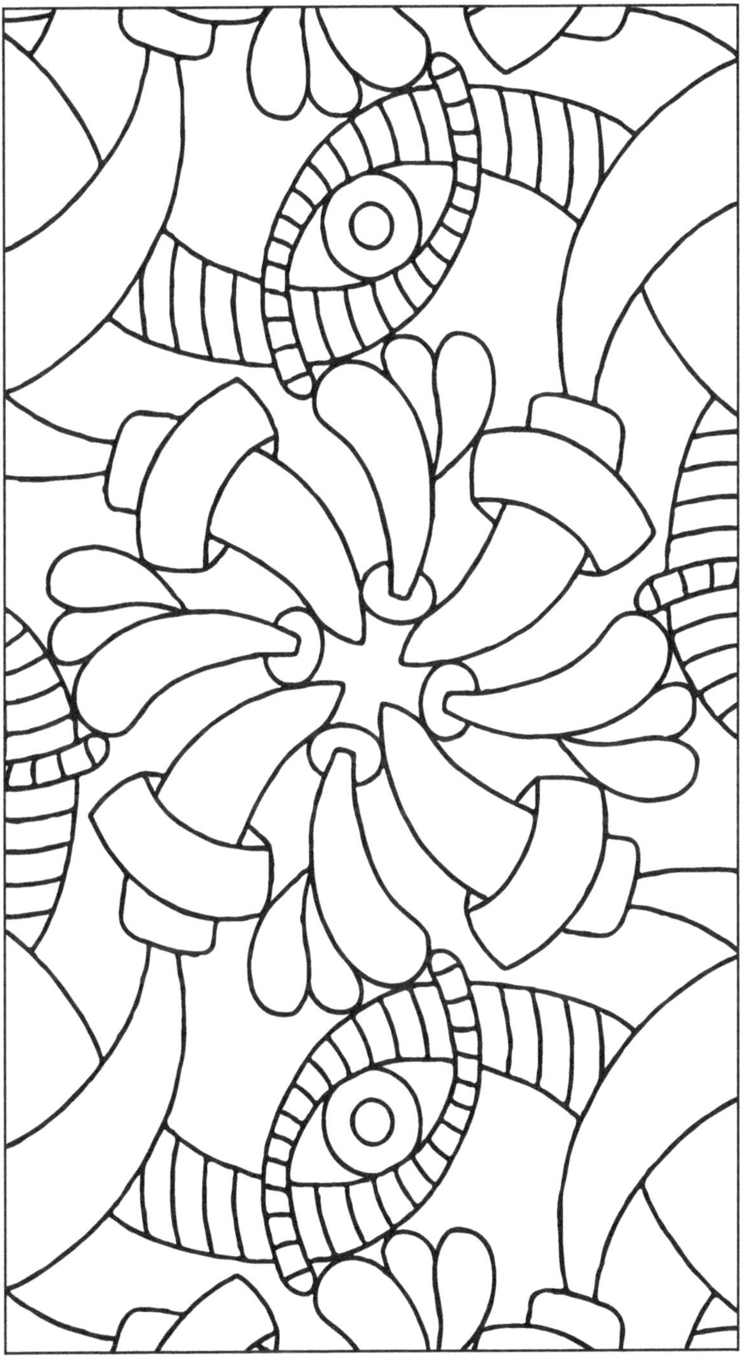

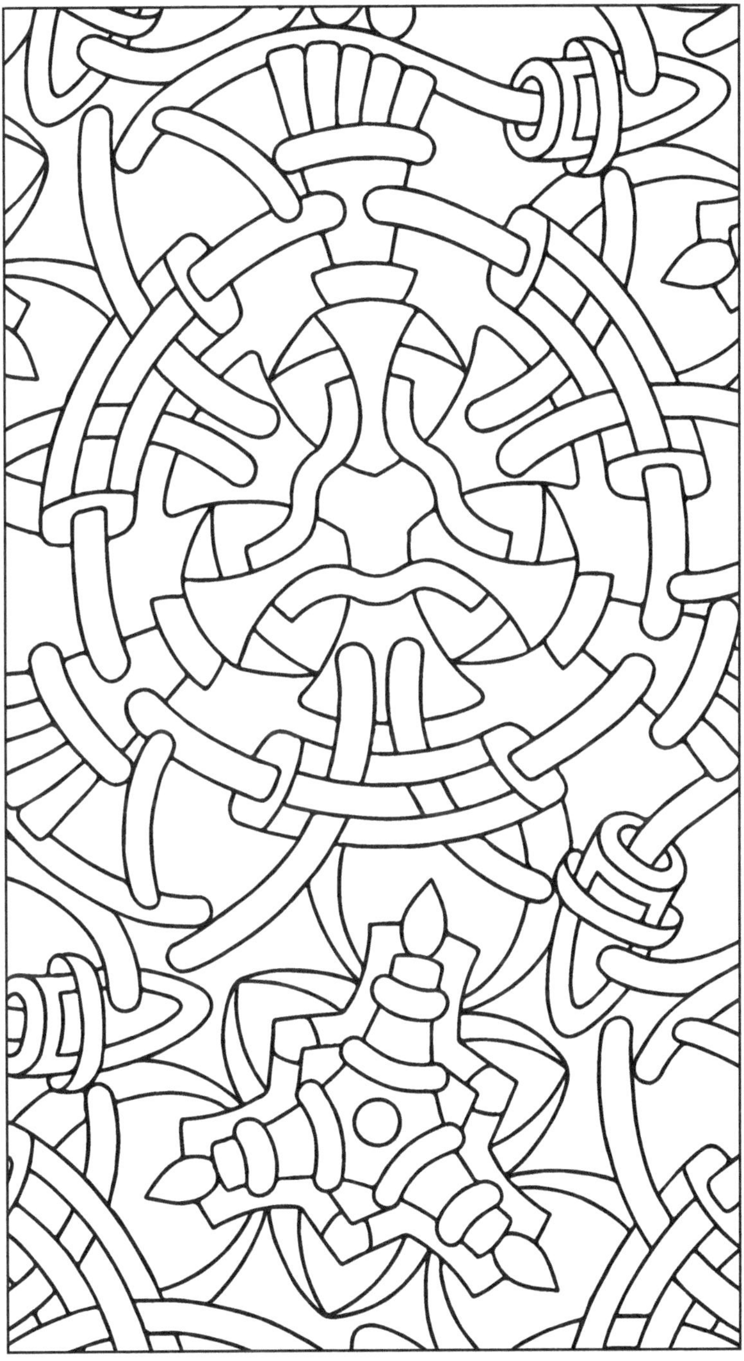

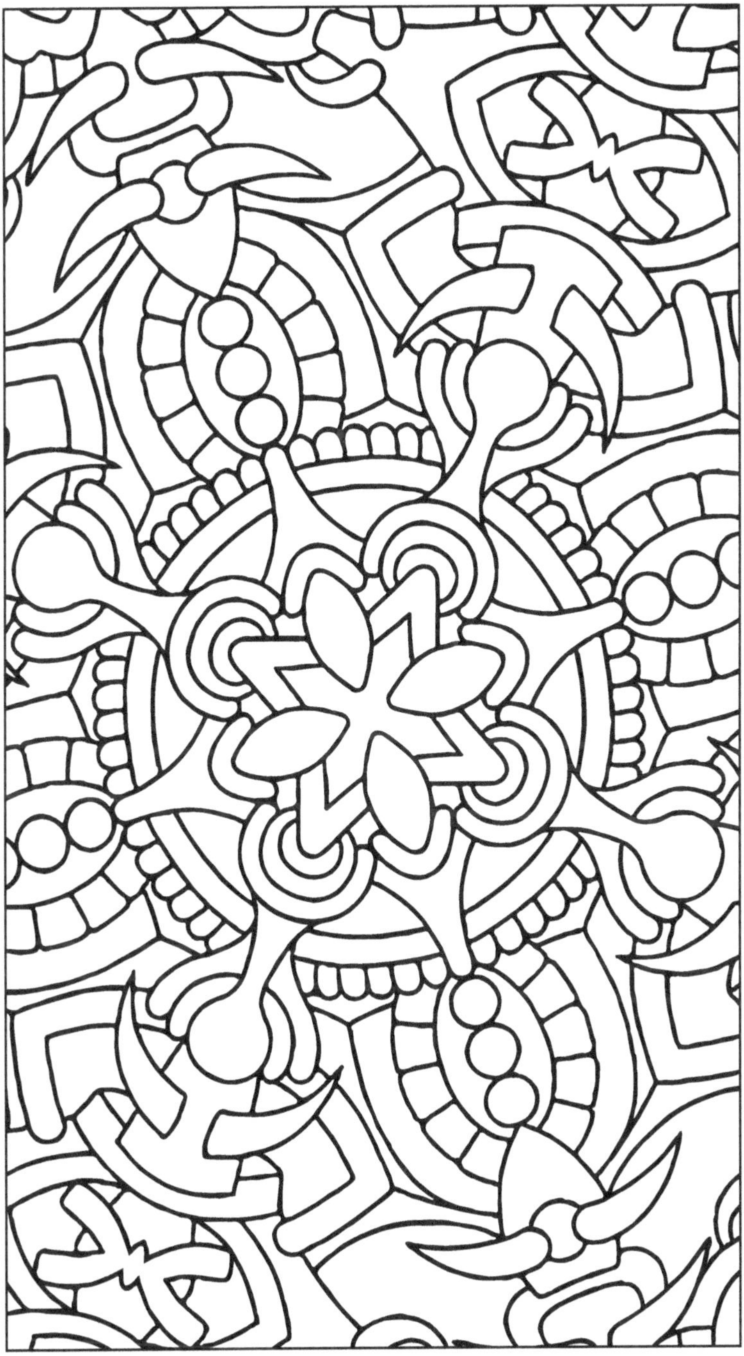

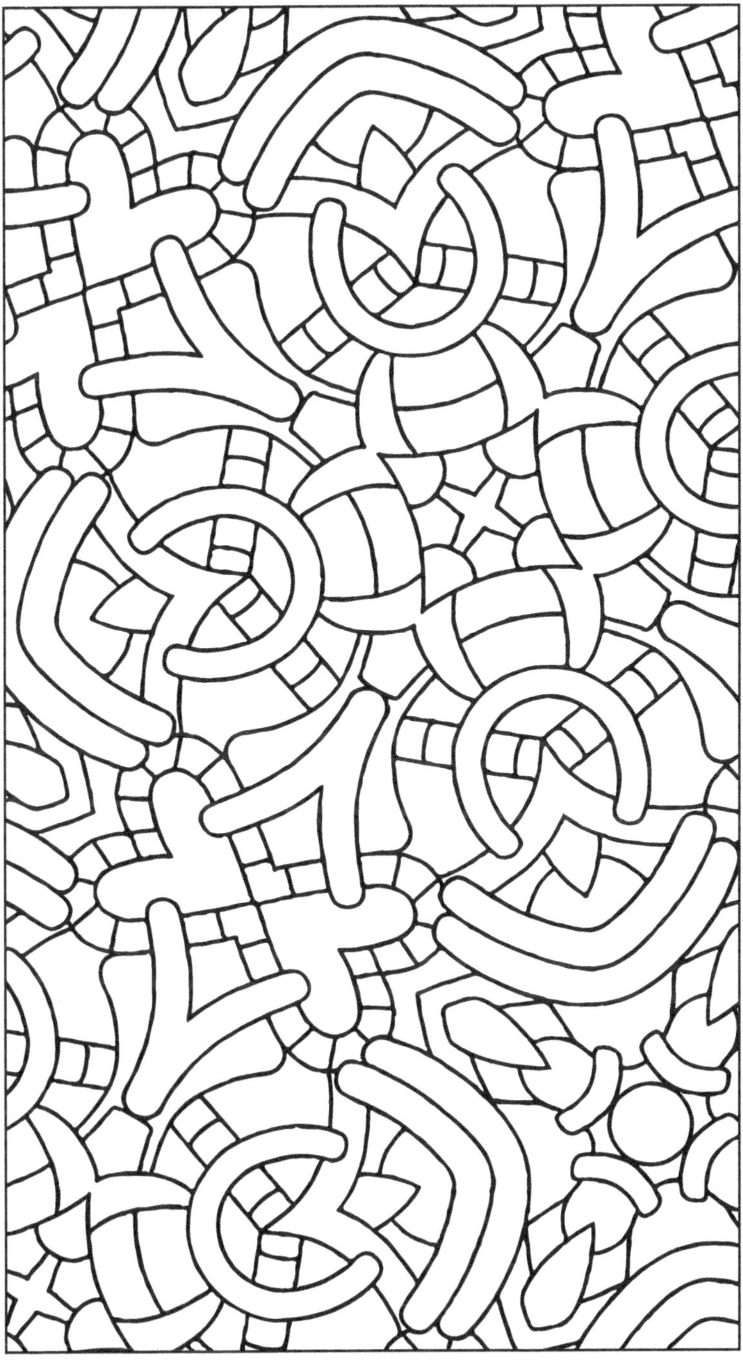

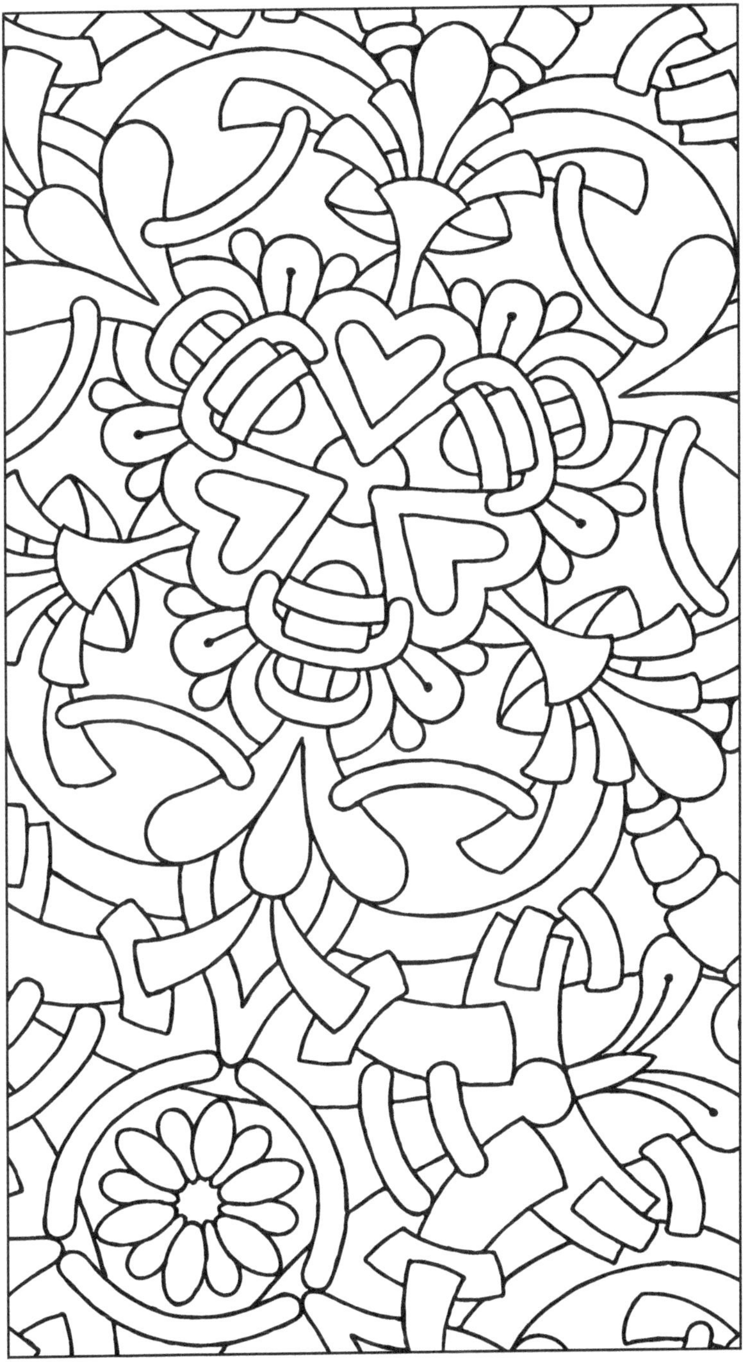

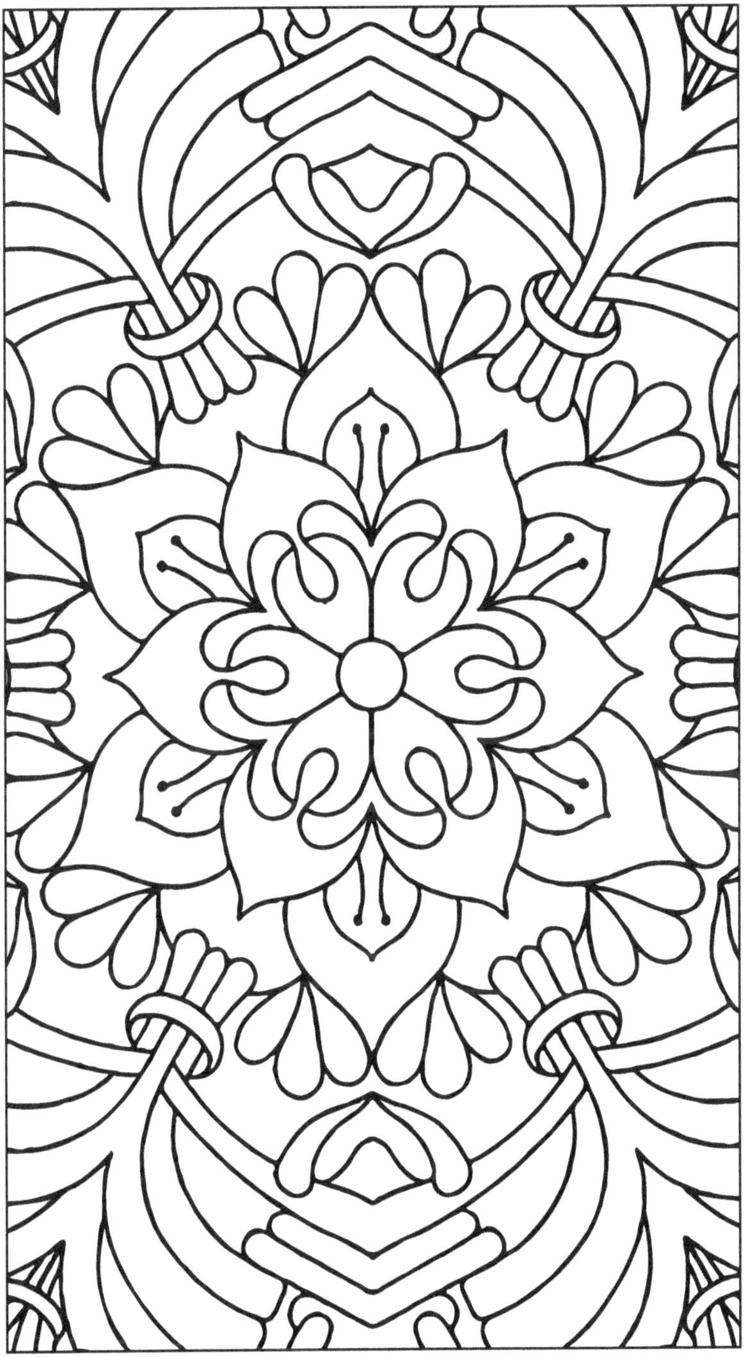

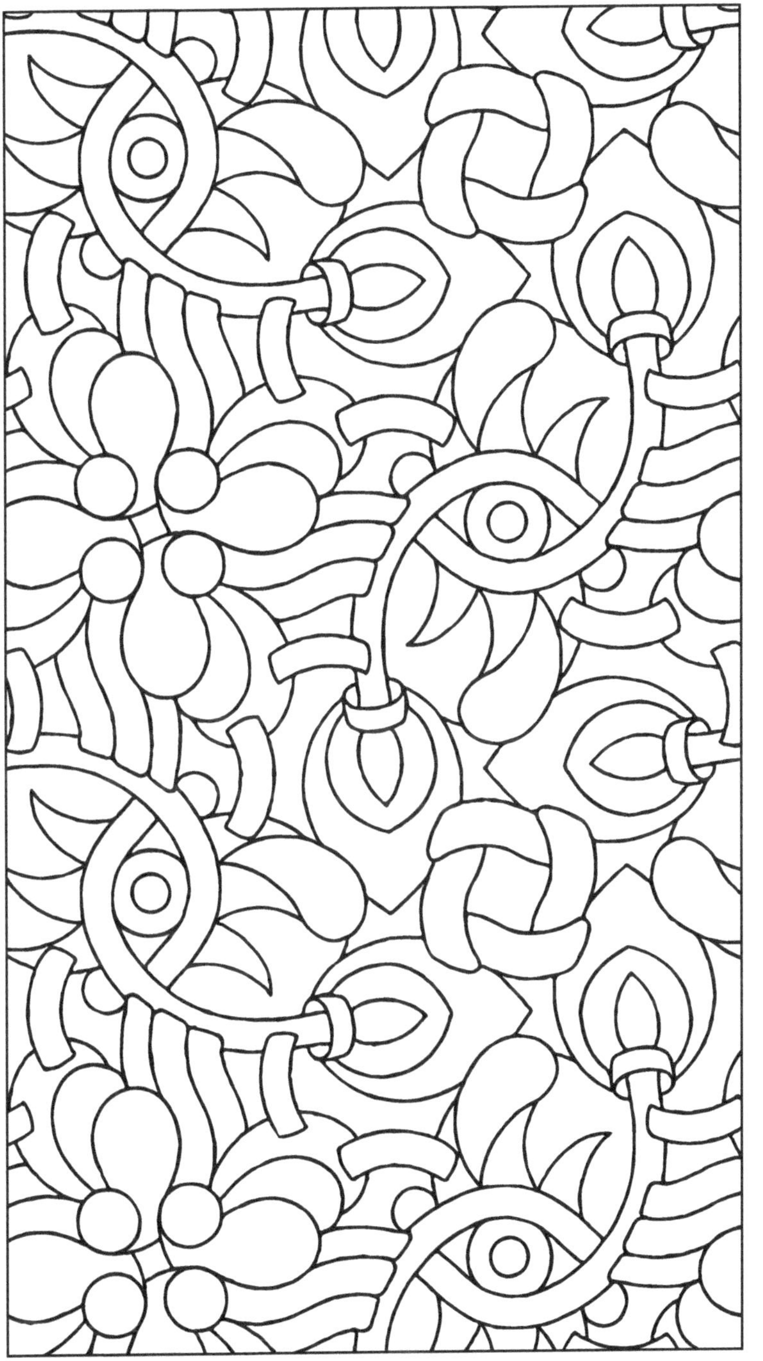

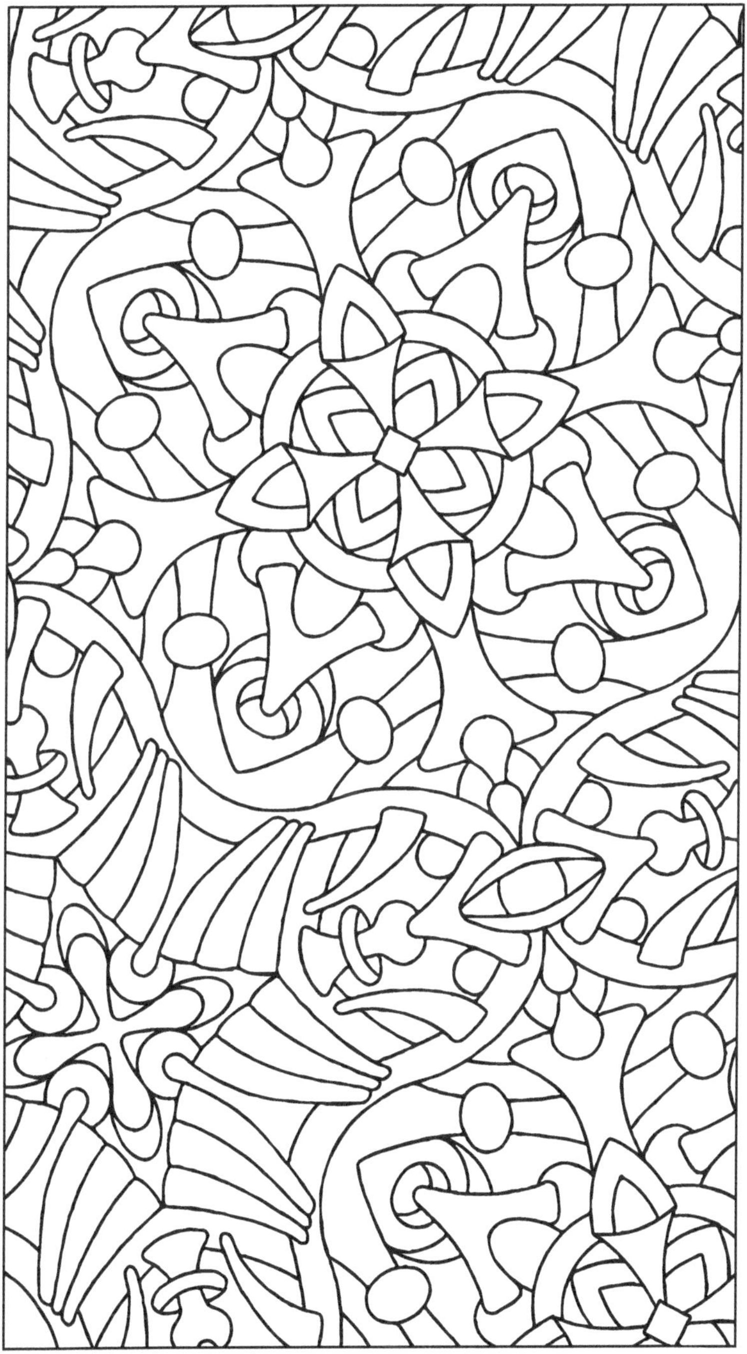

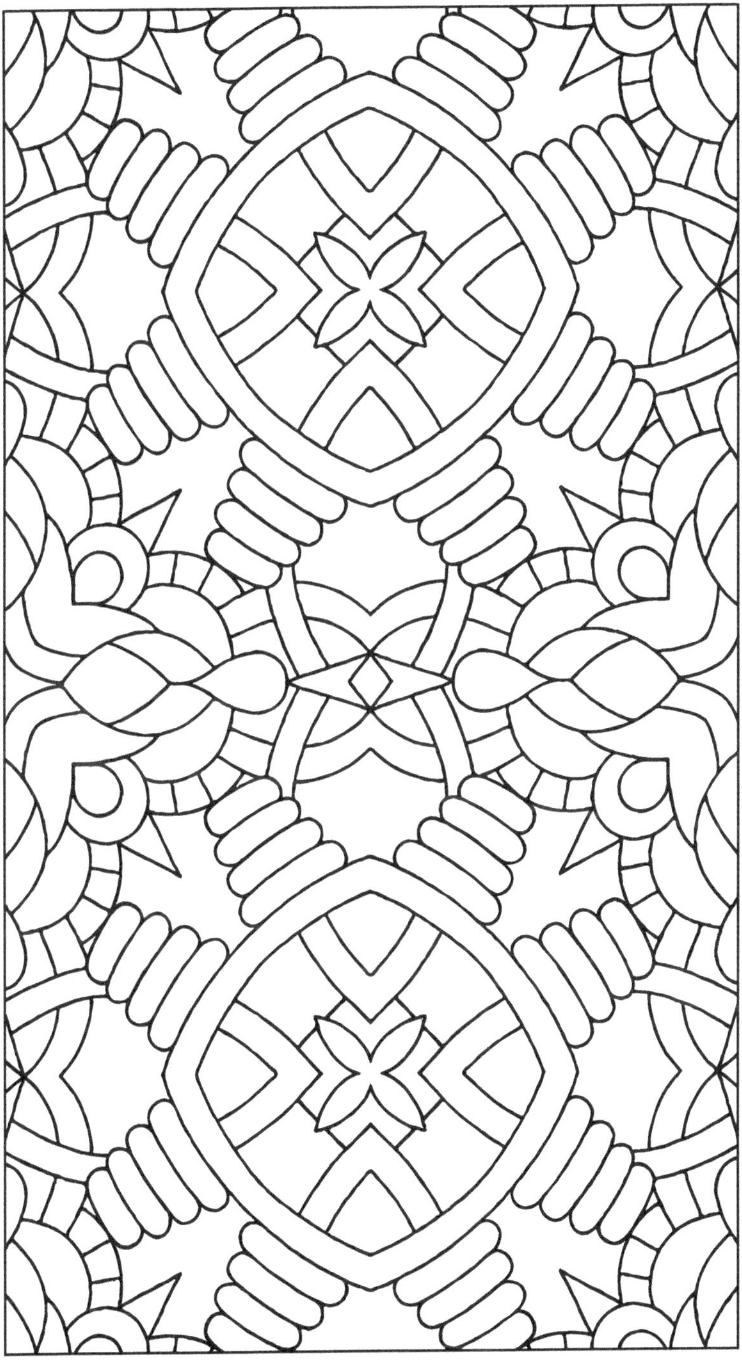

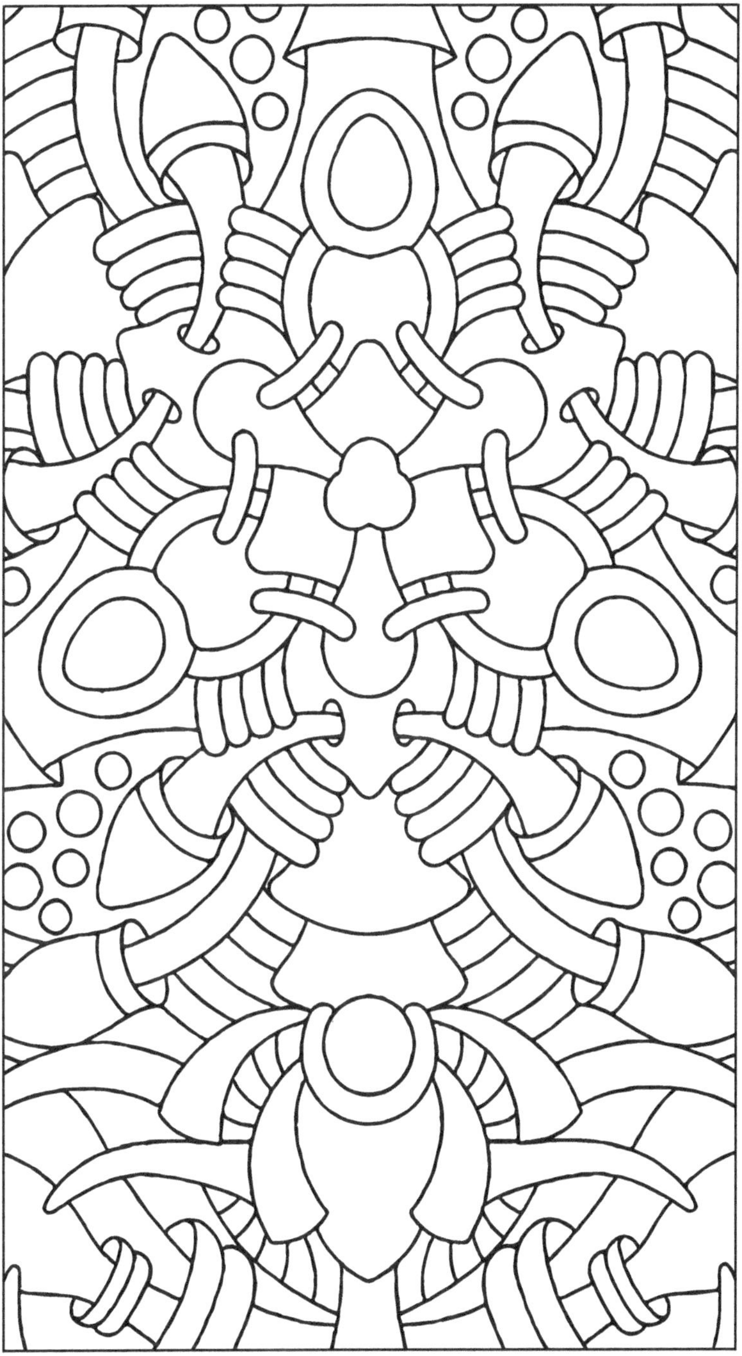

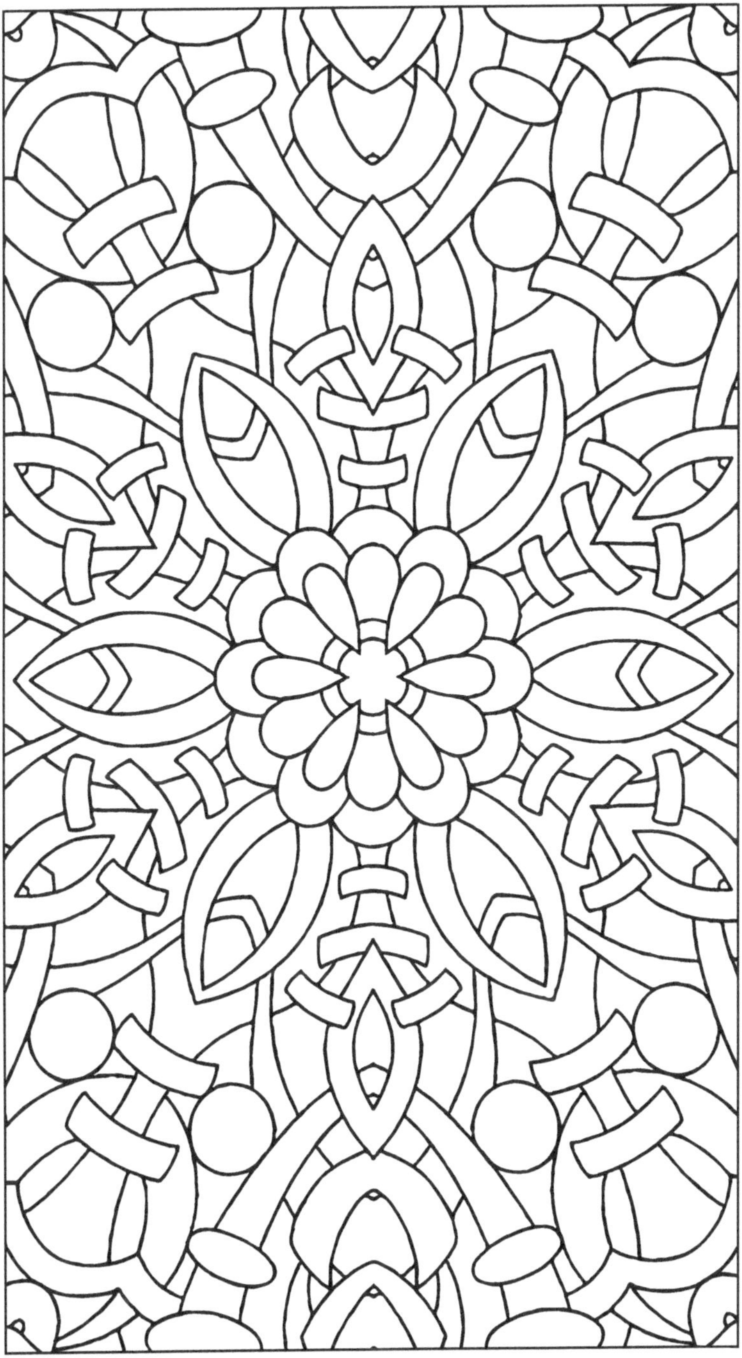

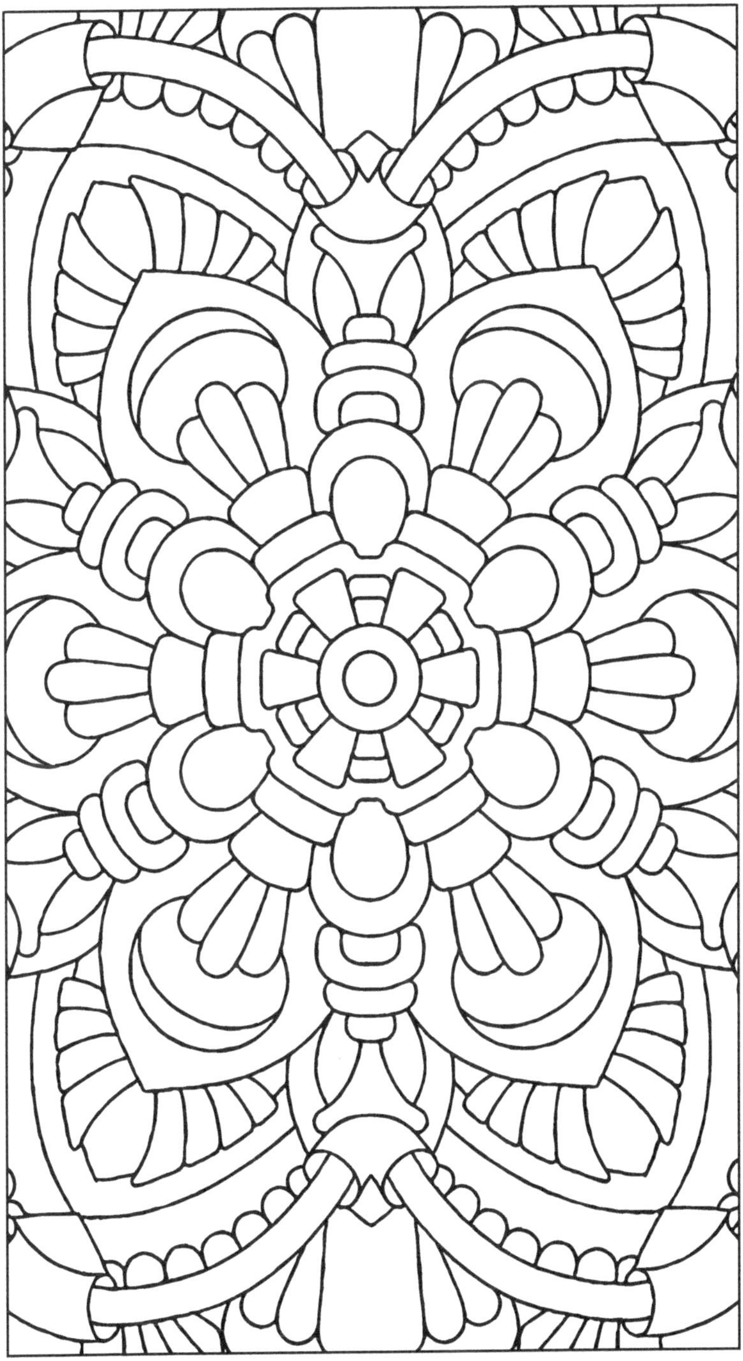

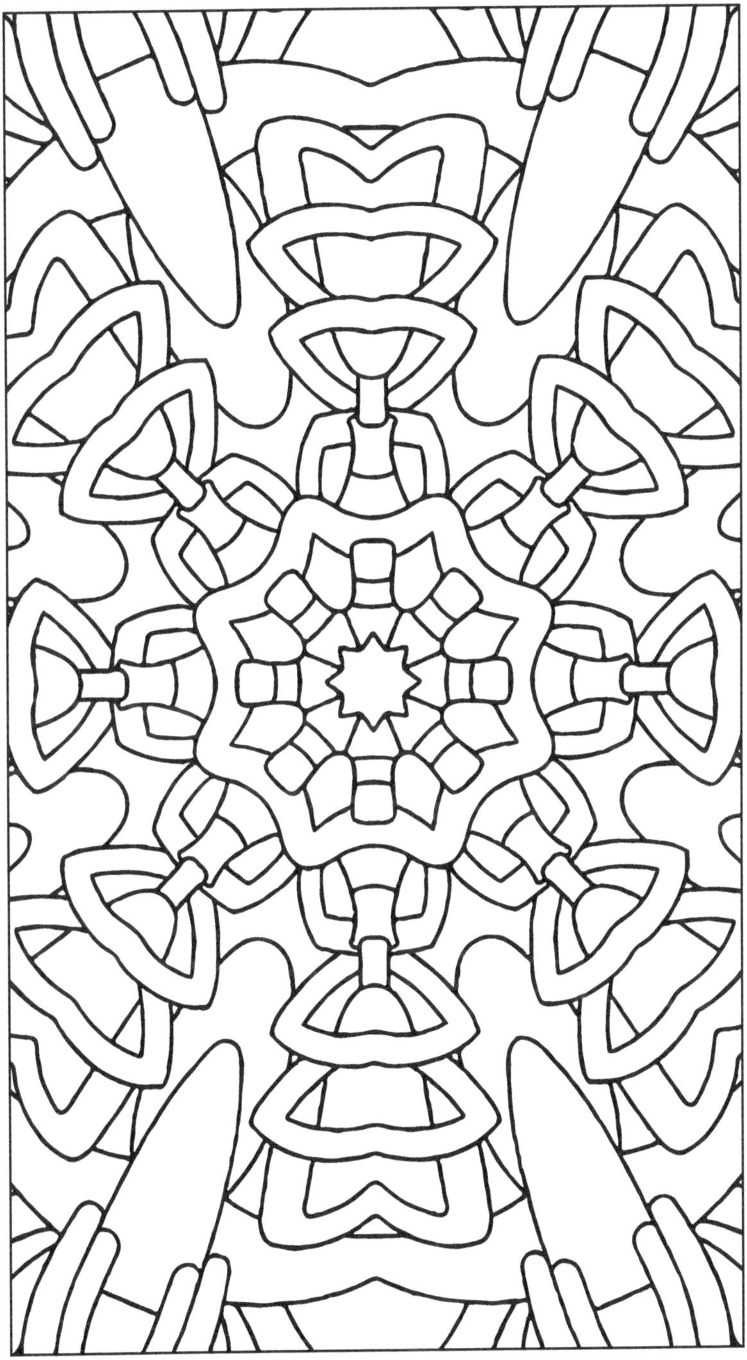

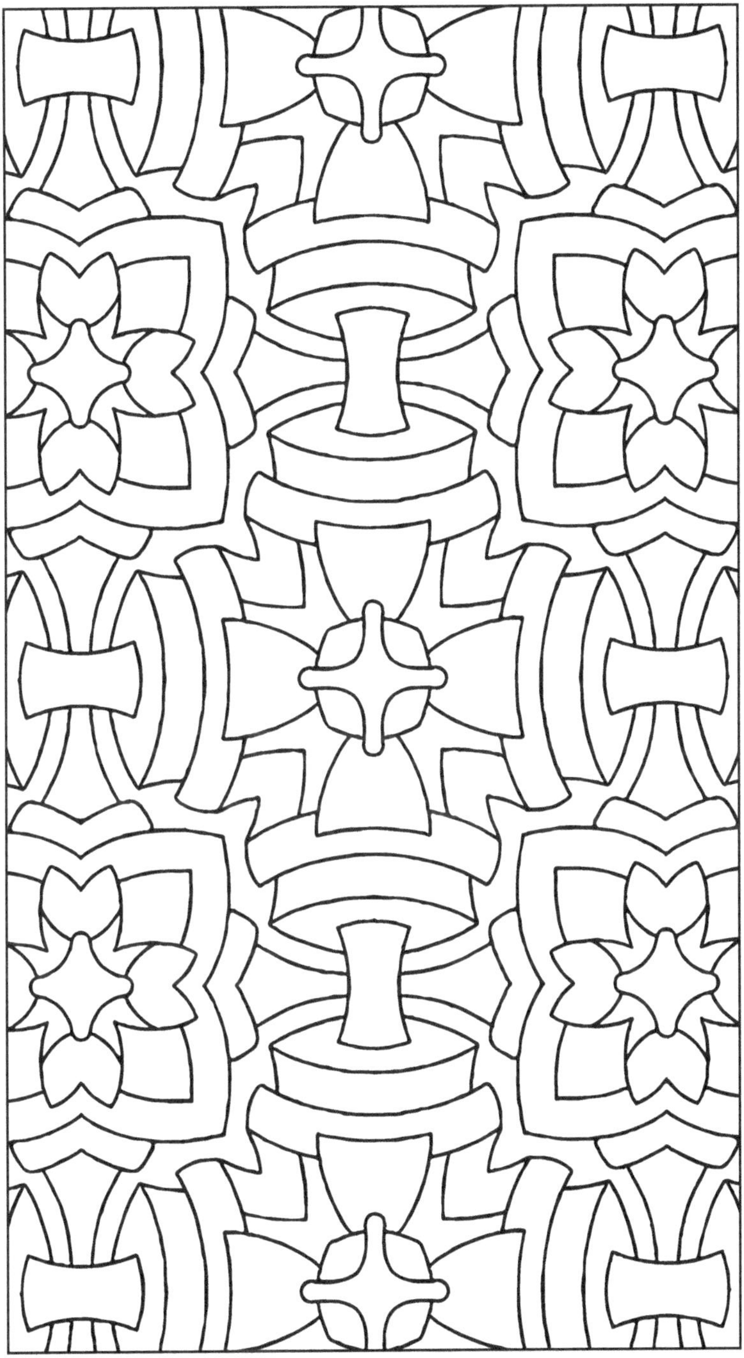

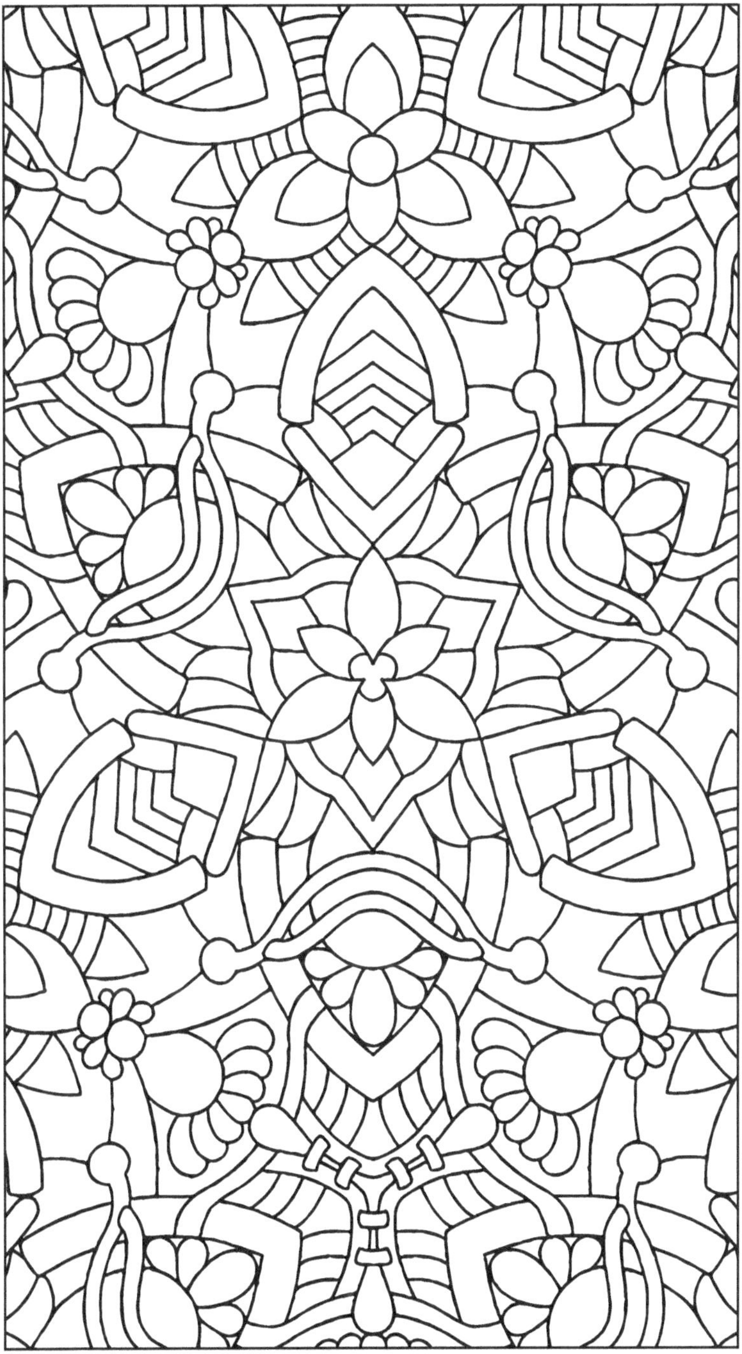

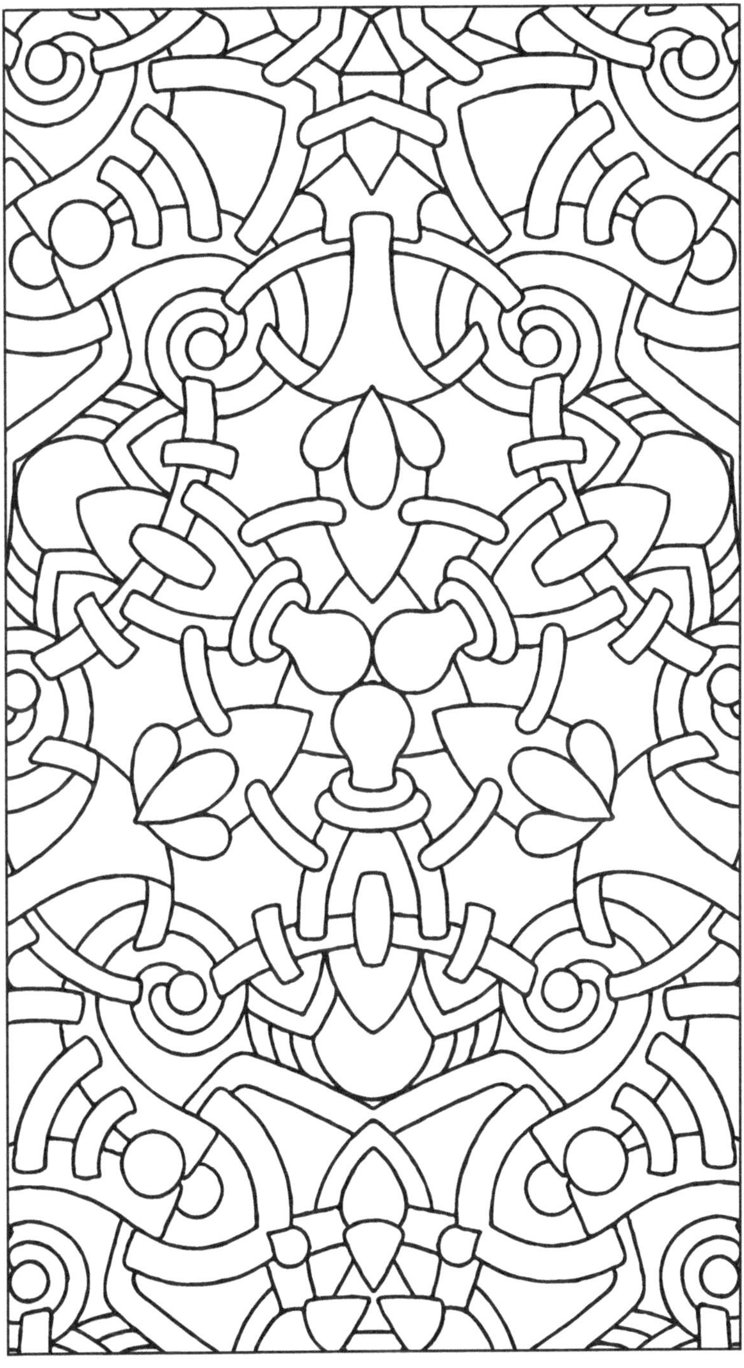

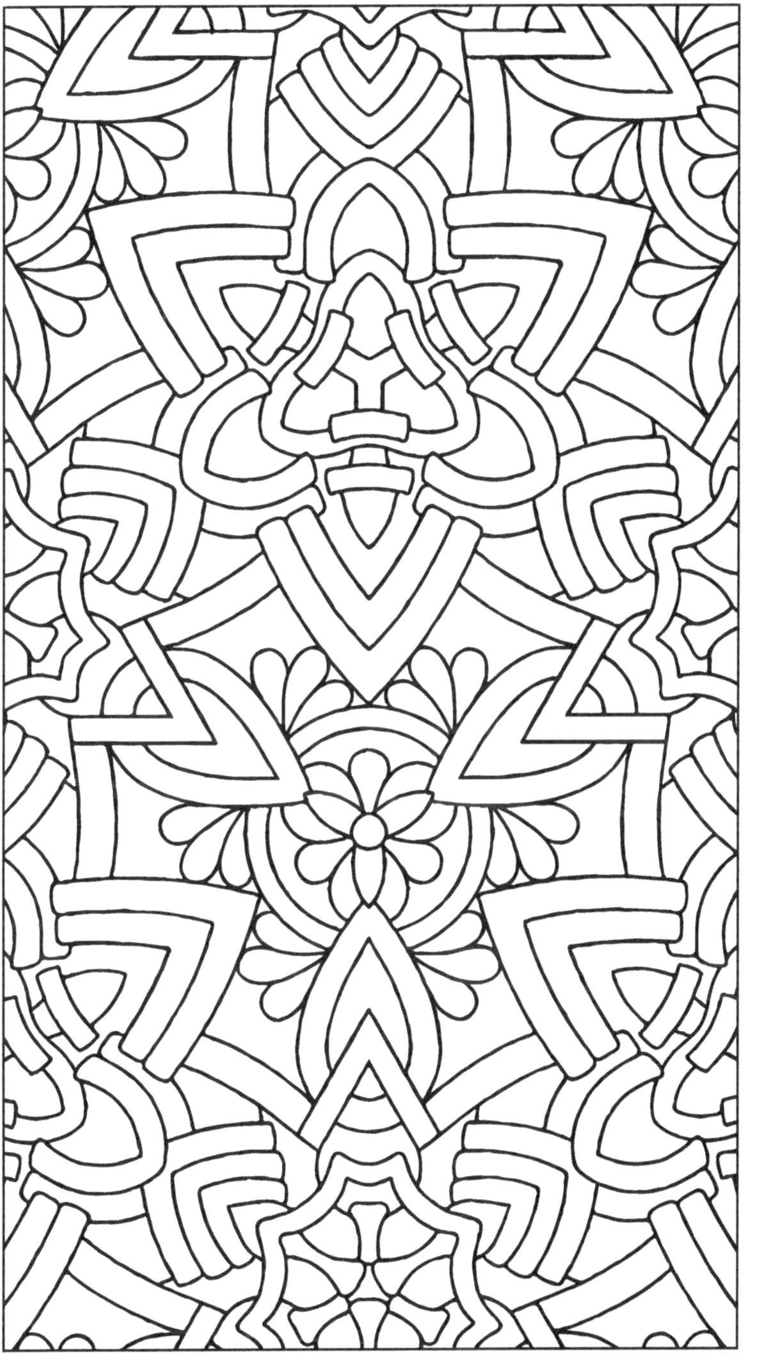

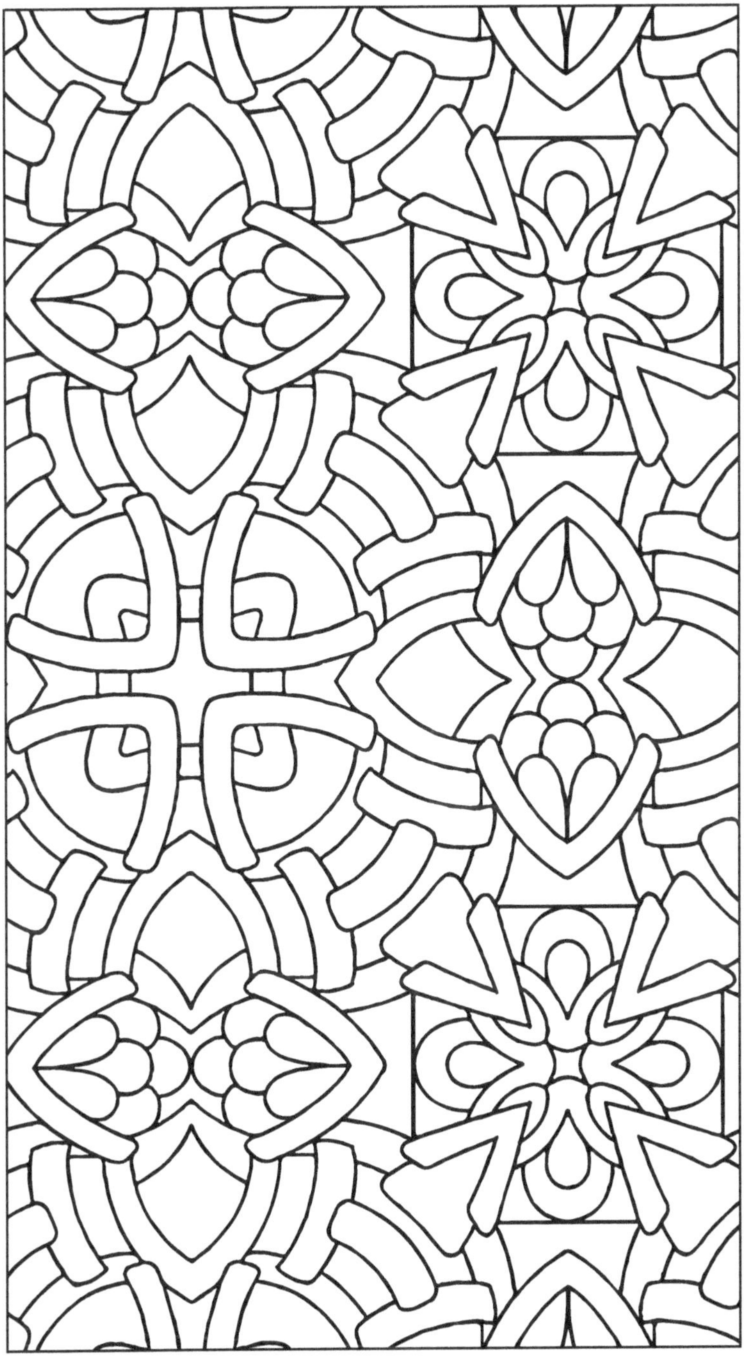

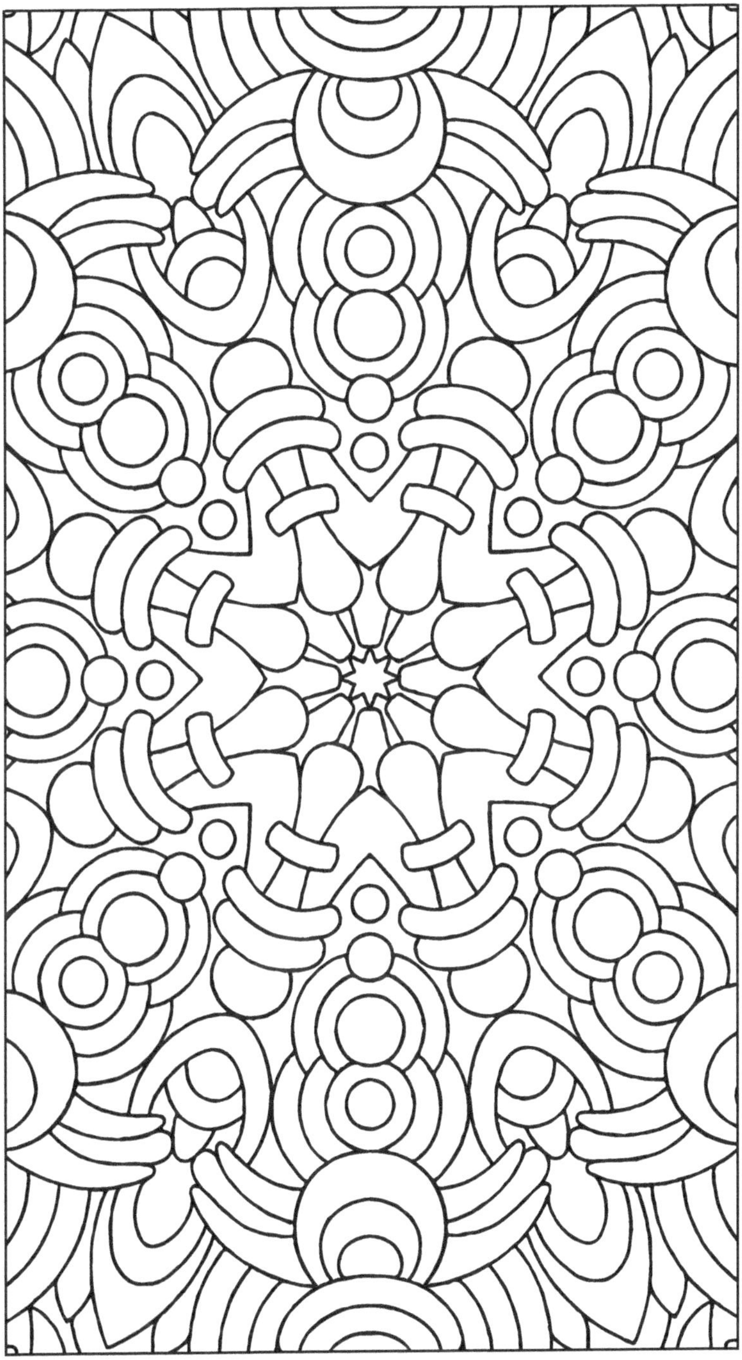

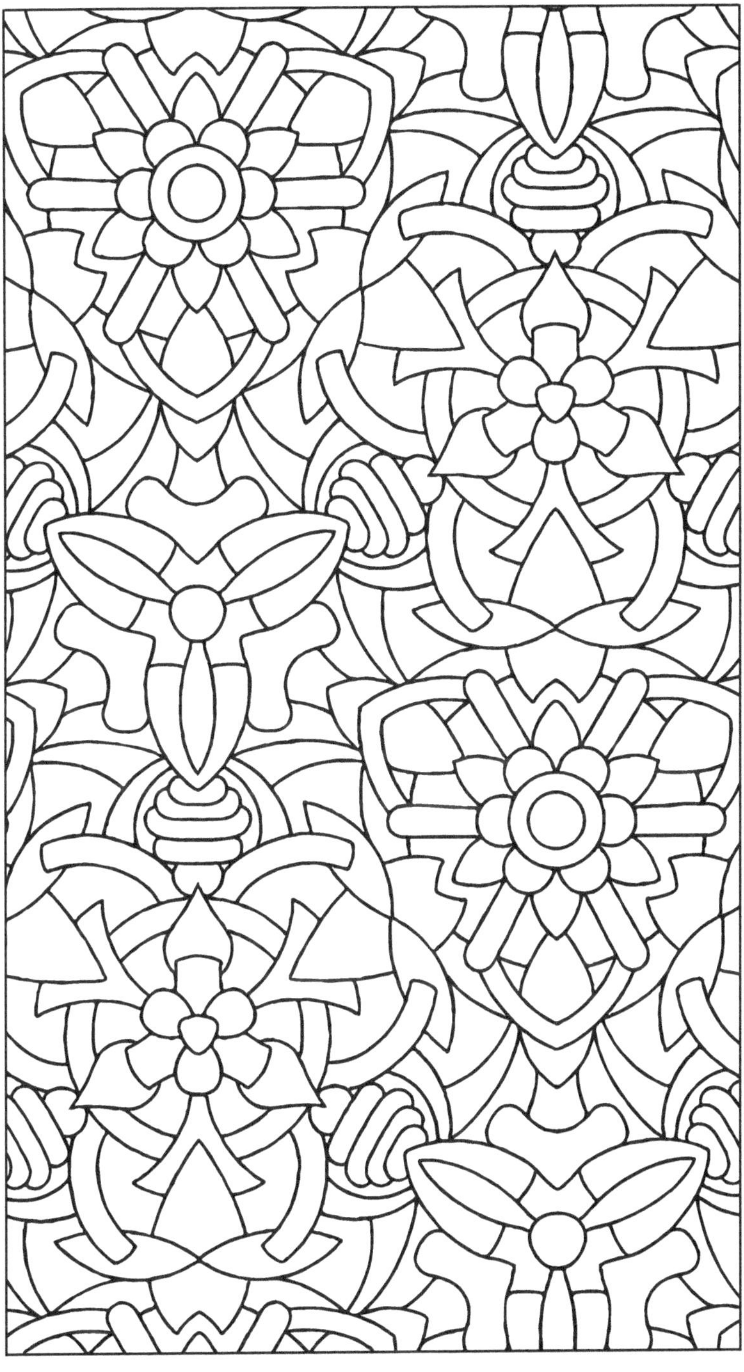

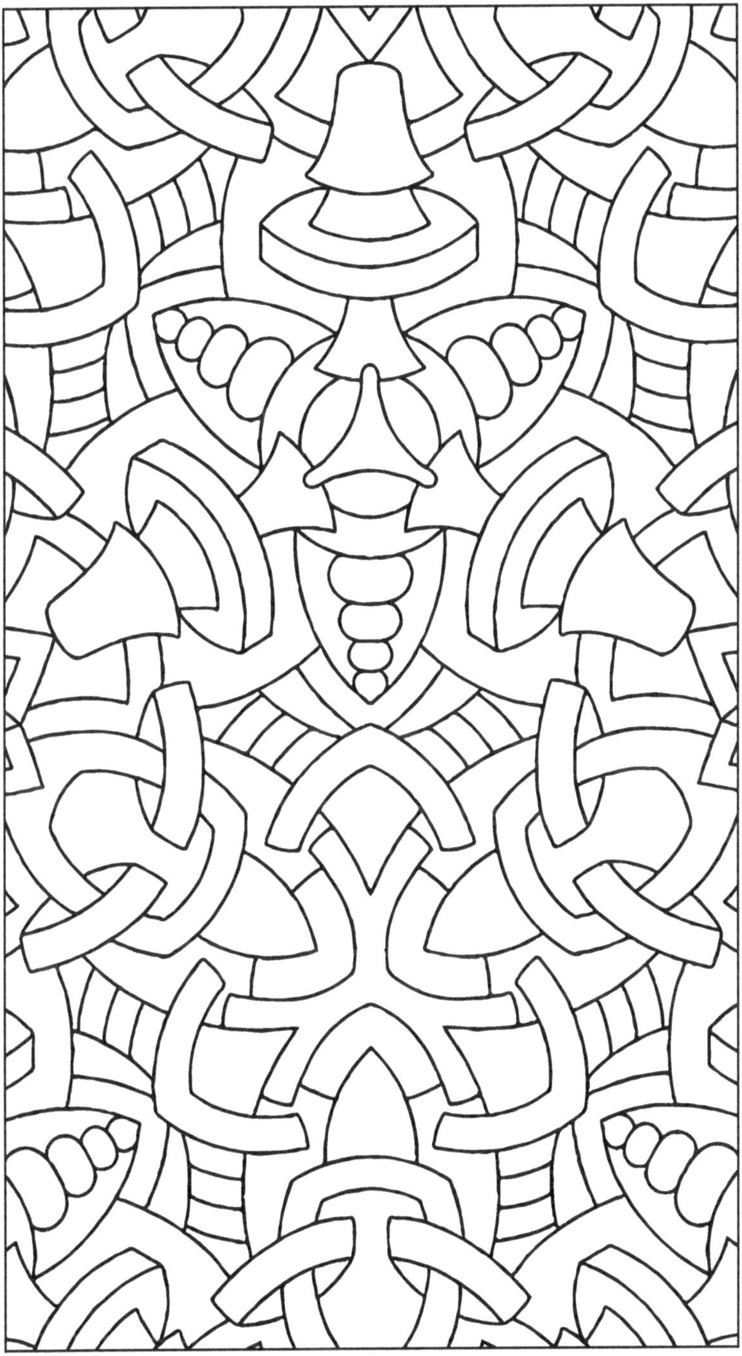

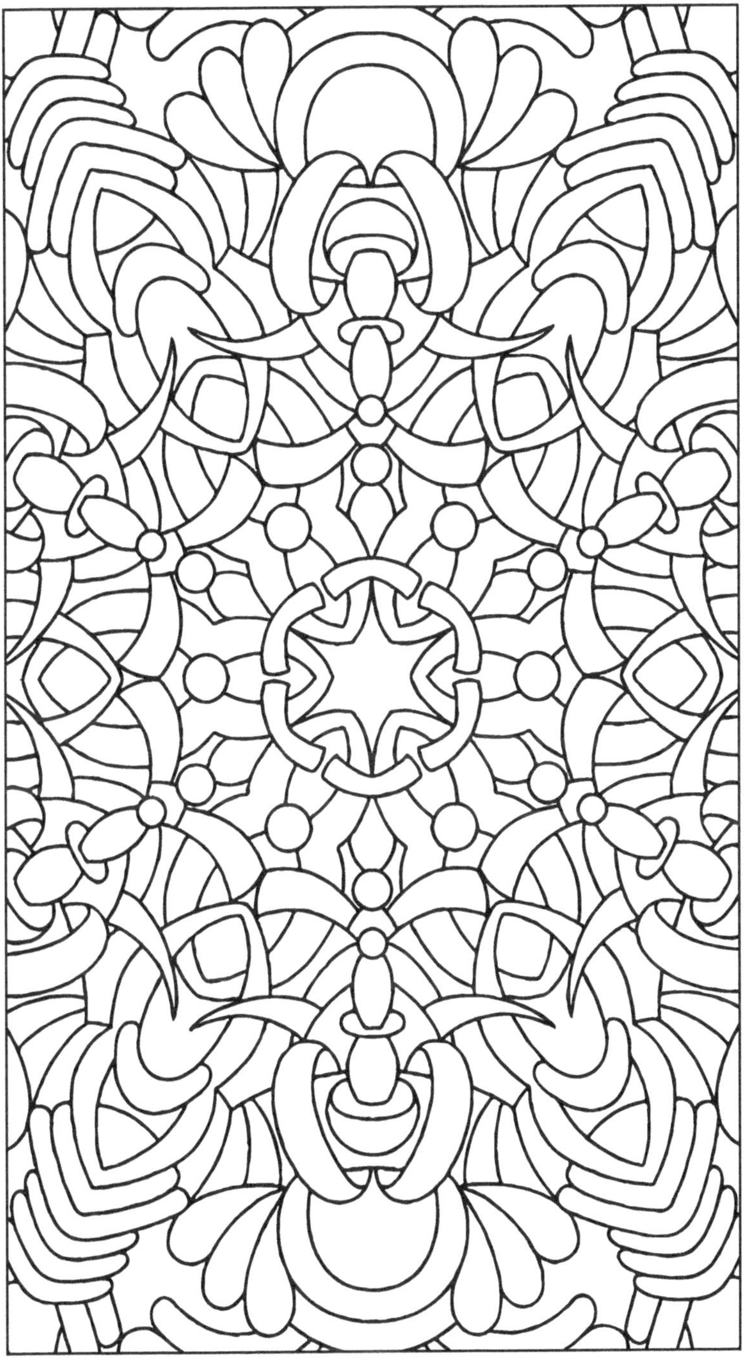

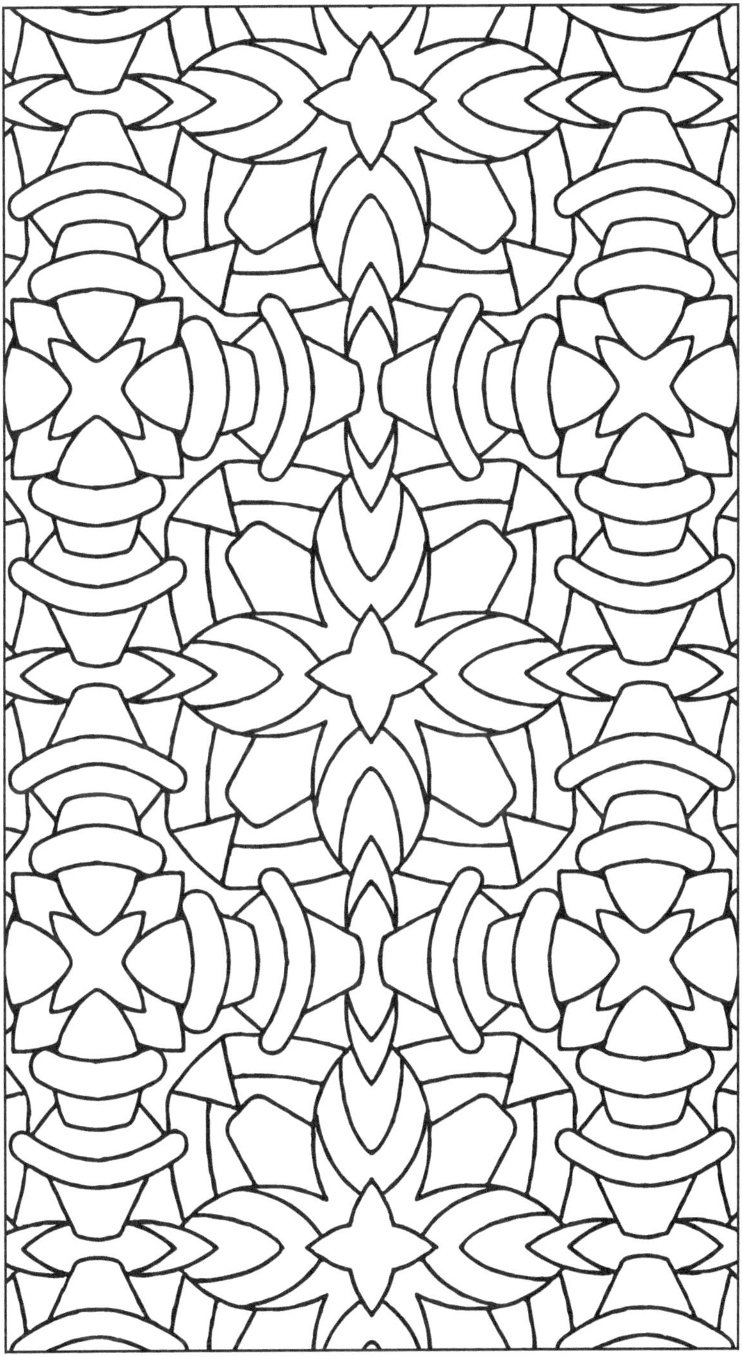

Also by Lori Greenberg

Mandala Coloring Books
Meditative Mandalas - Volume 1
Relaxing Mandalas - Volume 2
Calming Mandalas - Volume 3
Fanciful Mandalas - Volume 4

Pattern Coloring Books
Meditative Patterns - Volume 1
Relaxing Patterns - Volume 2
Calming Patterns - Volume 3

Pocket Pattern Coloring Books
Pocket Patterns - Volume 1
Relaxing Pocket Patterns - Volume 2

Large Space Pattern Coloring Books
Easy Patterns - Volume 1

Affirmation Coloring Books
Meditative Affirmations - Volume 1

Find these, and future books on Amazon

Visit **www.lorigreenberg.com**
and join Lori Greenberg's Coloring Connection
Facebook group for free coloring pages
and updates on new books.

www.ingramcontent.com/pod-product-compliance
Lightning Source LLC
Chambersburg PA
CBHW071215220526
45468CB00002B/614
9781974531592